Cambridge Elements

Elements in The Aegean Bronze Age
edited by
Carl Knappett
University of Toronto
Irene Nikolakopoulou
Hellenic Ministry of Culture, Archaeological Museum of Heraklion

SOCIAL CHANGE ACROSS THE END OF THE AEGEAN BRONZE AGE

Antonis Kotsonas
*Institute for the Study of the Ancient World,
New York University*

Shaftesbury Road, Cambridge CB2 8EA, United Kingdom

One Liberty Plaza, 20th Floor, New York, NY 10006, USA

477 Williamstown Road, Port Melbourne, VIC 3207, Australia

314–321, 3rd Floor, Plot 3, Splendor Forum, Jasola District Centre, New Delhi – 110025, India

103 Penang Road, #05–06/07, Visioncrest Commercial, Singapore 238467

Cambridge University Press is part of Cambridge University Press & Assessment, a department of the University of Cambridge.

We share the University's mission to contribute to society through the pursuit of education, learning and research at the highest international levels of excellence.

www.cambridge.org
Information on this title: www.cambridge.org/9781009455138

DOI: 10.1017/9781009455107

© Antonis Kotsonas 2025

This publication is in copyright. Subject to statutory exception and to the provisions of relevant collective licensing agreements, no reproduction of any part may take place without the written permission of Cambridge University Press & Assessment.

When citing this work, please include a reference to the DOI 10.1017/9781009455107

First published 2025

A catalogue record for this publication is available from the British Library

ISBN 978-1-009-45513-8 Hardback
ISBN 978-1-009-45509-1 Paperback
ISSN 2754-2998 (online)
ISSN 2754-298X (print)

Cambridge University Press & Assessment has no responsibility for the persistence or accuracy of URLs for external or third-party internet websites referred to in this publication and does not guarantee that any content on such websites is, or will remain, accurate or appropriate.

For EU product safety concerns, contact us at Calle de José Abascal, 56, 1°, 28003 Madrid, Spain, or email eugpsr@cambridge.org

Social Change across the End of the Aegean Bronze Age

Elements in The Aegean Bronze Age

DOI: 10.1017/9781009455107
First published online: December 2025

Antonis Kotsonas
Institute for the Study of the Ancient World, New York University
Author for correspondence: Antonis Kotsonas, ak7509@nyu.edu

Abstract: For a long time, scholarship on the end of the Aegean Bronze Age has been preoccupied with political, ethnic/racial, economic, environmental, and other change; however, it has rarely centered the discussion on social change. Drawing from anthropological and sociological critiques of social change, the Element compares the Greek archaeological record before and after the collapse of 1200 BCE, focusing on developments in the 12th to early 10th centuries, which are examined against the background of the Mycenaean palatial system of the 14th and 13th centuries. The seven sections of the Element cover the reasons for the collapse of the Mycenaean palaces; socio-political, demographic, and socio-economic change after the collapse; and the manifestation of this change in settlements, burials, and sanctuaries. The Appendix offers a discussion of the relative and absolute chronologies of the period, with emphasis on recent important but debatable suggestions for revisions.

Keywords: Aegean, Bronze Age, Early Iron Age, Social Change, Collapse

© Antonis Kotsonas 2025

ISBNs: 9781009455138 (HB), 9781009455091 (PB), 9781009455107 (OC)
ISSNs: 2754-2998 (online), 2754-298X (print)

Contents

1 Introduction — 1

2 The Collapse of the Mycenaean Palaces — 4

3 Socio-Political Change — 10

4 Demography and Social Change — 16

5 Socio-Economic Change, and Exchange — 19

6 Settlements and Social Change — 29

7 Burials and Social Change — 37

8 Sanctuaries and Social Change — 43

9 Conclusions — 49

   Appendix: Chronology — 50

   References — 56

1 Introduction

The end of the Aegean Bronze Age is traditionally visualized either through old paintings (and now AI-generated visuals) showing ancient cities ablaze, or maps of the Eastern Mediterranean which plot migrations and invasions. Such drama occasionally permeates its scholarship, though for the most part it maintains a sober outlook on this historical watershed (Dickinson 2006; Lemos & Kotsonas 2020; Cline 2021; 2024). Against this backdrop, I welcomed the editors' invitation to discuss the end of the Aegean Bronze Age through the lens of social change. Change has long preoccupied archaeology (Crellin 2021), and scholarship on the end of the Aegean Bronze Age has discussed widely political, ethnic/racial, economic, environmental and other change; however, this scholarship has rarely focused on social change. A few titles mention the term (Dierckx 1986; Philippa-Touchais 2011), but their authors do not engage with it. A recent monograph makes recurrent references to the concept (Knodell 2021: *passim*), but does not problematize it. The same issue is identifiable in titles that reference social change and cover other periods of Greek antiquity (Small 2011; Wiersma & Voutsaki 2016), which can be traced back to the late 1980s, and multiplied in the last two decades, as confirmed by a term search of the Nestor bibliographic database (May 2025).

To gain a broader appreciation of social change and the critique it has attracted, it is useful to turn to other disciplines, especially anthropology (e.g., Mair 1969; Heyman 2005; Chase-Dunn & Lerro 2014) and sociology (e.g., Moore 1963; Noble 2000; Vago 2004). Sociologists understand social change as encompassing developments in the structure and functioning of society, and variation in social relationships over time – precisely the topics of the present study. The same scholars, however, provide varied and occasionally conflicting definitions for these concepts (Vago 2004: 7–10). For current purpose, social change is understood as "the restructuring of human social institutions: culture, consciousness, technology, organizations, settlement systems, forms of exchange and structures of authority and decision making" (Chase-Dunn & Babones 2006: 1). These different aspects of social change are addressed in the following sections, though a few (e.g. consciousness or decision making) receive limited attention because of the paucity of primary evidence.

Anthropologists have leveled the criticism that discussions of social change often stem from the flawed assumption that "stasis is normal and that only change needs explanation," and they have scorned the tendency of scholars to approach historical development through transitions from one stage of cultural evolution to another (Heyman 2005; cf. Crellin 2021: 6–10). This critique is particularly relevant to Aegean archaeology, since notions of cultural evolution manifest themselves in the periodization that distinguishes between a Bronze Age and an Iron Age. These two periods are part of the time-honored three-age system of prehistory, the conceptual underpinnings of which are increasingly called into question (Crellin 2021: 6–7, 17–19; Pare 2025: 285–300). The same critiques apply to alternative periodizations, including the one which distinguishes between a Mycenaean Palatial and a Postpalatial period in the late 2nd millennium (for chronology and periodization, see Appendix), or those featured in titles such as *Palace to Polis* (Lemos 2005), *Citadel to City-State* (Thomas & Conant 1999), or *From Wanax to Basileus* (Deger-Jalkotzy & Lemos 2006; cf. Crielaard 2011; Bettelli 2015). Less relevant to the study of the Late Bronze Age (LBA) to Early Iron Age (EIA) transition is the anthropological criticism that the emphasis on social change offers a one-sided historical perspective, which suppresses the possibility of stability (Heyman 2005). In the Aegean case, both "change" and "continuity" have attracted much attention (see e.g. the titles of Prent 2005; Dickinson 2006; Bulmer 2020; Lupack 2020), and have occasionally been politicized (Kotsonas 2016: 261) in ways which recall broader anthropological discourses between "continuationists" and "transformationists" (Chase-Dunn & Lerro 2014: 12).

To analyze social change across the end of the Bronze Age in the succinct format of a *Cambridge Element*, one must make hard choices over the scope of the work. Accordingly, I focus the discussion on the developments from the twelfth to early tenth centuries, which I set against the background of the Mycenaean Palatial period of the fourteenth and thirteenth centuries, making only select references to earlier or later periods. This approach is familiar to Aegeanists (e.g. Dickinson 2006) and fits the context of a *Cambridge Elements* series on the Aegean Bronze Age. However, the apposition and opposition of the two periods runs the risk of characterizing the later period not as what it was, but as what it was not, that is, as a period missing palatial political, social, economic, material, and other trappings. To mitigate this problem, I balance the current emphasis on the Bronze Age collapse with discussions of the resilience of Aegean communities (see next section); I draw from recent work that treats the Aegean twelfth century as a distinct phase involving varied responses to palatial landscapes and material worlds and novel developments in society and culture (Thomatos 2006; van Damme 2017); I challenge a range of gloomy notions for the period ca. 1000 BCE; and I problematize their empirical basis and theoretical underpinnings. The seven sections below cover: the reasons for the collapse of ca. 1200 BCE; socio-political, demographic, and socio-economic change; and the manifestation of this change in settlements, burials, and sanctuaries (thus echoing the definition of social change provided above). The Appendix offers a discussion of the relative and absolute chronologies of the period, with emphasis on recent proposals for revisions which potentially have major implications for historical narratives of the period but remain controversial.

Because of limitations of space, this work cannot do full justice to the wide-ranging fieldwork results, regional historical trajectories, and classes of material culture; however, these important aspects receive lengthy analyses in Lemos and Kotsonas 2020 (and material culture looms large in other works of mine: Kotsonas 2008a; 2012; 2024). Instead, I structure my analysis around major debates surrounding the end of the Aegean Bronze Age, and on quantitative and qualitative arguments about social change (cf. Chase-Dunn & Lerro 2014: 12). In pursuing a discursive approach, this Element very much echoes the structure of graduate seminars which I have taught on the topic, and reflects my interest in historiography (e.g. Kotsonas 2016). Also, I draw inspiration from Oliver Dickinson's (2006) textbook on the period, especially from the excellent introductions to his different chapters (praised in Kotsonas 2008b). Most relevant literature focuses on the central and southern Aegean, but the northern part of the area and sites and regions along the Ionian Sea also receive attention in my analysis (Figure 1).

Figure 1 Map of the Aegean with sites of the Palatial and Postpalatial periods mentioned in the text. Courtesy of Dominic Pollard.

My selective coverage of the enormous literature on the topic seeks to find a balance between seminal studies, especially of the 1960s and 1970s, and the latest research capturing current developments in the field. I hope that the scope of the work will stimulate nonexperts to dig deeper into the end of the Bronze Age, while also offering fresh insights for those familiar with the material.

2 The Collapse of the Mycenaean Palaces

In recent years, a few scholars have revived the old idea (e.g., Desborough 1964: 218) that Mycenaean Greece was a unified state, like the Hittite empire of Anatolia, and should be identified with the kingdom of Ahhiyawa mentioned in Hittite texts (Kelder 2010; Eder & Jung 2015; Wiener 2017: 61–2). However, this idea has faced much criticism (Dickinson 2006: 26–9; Maran & Wright 2020: 113; Galaty & Parkinson 2025), and the Mycenaean world is widely conceived of as a conglomeration of polities scattered around the southern and central Aegean, and linked in networks of alliance and dependency (Maran & Wright 2020: 112–7; cf. Dickinson 2006: 24–41; Galaty & Parkinson 2007; van Wijngaarden & Driessen 2022). Mycenaean polities were controlled by towns, which were small by Near Eastern standards, and from the fourteenth century (Late Helladic (LH) IIIA)) they were centered on a palace. The core of the Mycenaean palace was a building of standard tripartite form (megaron), with those of Mycenae, Pylos, and Tiryns exhibiting remarkable similarities in architectural layout and iconographic programs by the thirteenth century (LH IIIB). Although the Linear B tablets found in the palaces yield almost no information on political history, diplomatic relations and long-distance trade, they are taken to demonstrate that the various palatial polities were autonomous and controlled a territory of considerable extent; for example, the palace of Pylos came to control most of Messenia through territorial expansion (Cosmopoulos 2019), while the palace of Thebes ruled over much of eastern Boeotia and southern Euboea. The tablets document a clear socio-political hierarchy: Each palatial polity was ruled by a *wanax*, who held profane and sacred authority, and commanded a military, political, religious, and administrative apparatus. The *wanax* is hard to pin down in the archaeological record of the Palatial period (Olsen 2020: 297), unlike earlier Mycenaean rulers who received lavish and/or monumental graves. Both the textual and the archaeological record from Mycenaean Greece suggest that the palaces employed and commanded numerous and varied craftsmen and other specialists (Galaty & Parkinson

2007), controlled wide-ranging economic activities, and collected taxation from the local communities (*damoi*) within their territory.

At around ca. 1200 BCE, conflagrations consumed the palaces of Tiryns, Pylos, Mycenae, and Thebes – and many urban centers around the Eastern Mediterranean – and the Mycenaean palatial system collapsed (e.g. Dickinson 2006; Middleton 2010; 2020; Lemos & Kotsonas 2020; Cline 2021; but see the critical approach of Millek 2023). By a recent estimate, scholarship has proposed 26 different reasons for this collapse (Middleton 2020: 13, table 2.1). Most scholars prefer to lump many of these together, as do I in the following review, which is organized to reflect historiographic development (a parameter often neglected in other such reviews). By investigating the role of various agents in generating and responding to the collapse, the different hypotheses promote different strands of interpretation for social and other change across the end of the Bronze Age, as explained in the different sections that follow.

Explanations for the collapse of the Mycenaean palaces were once sought in ancient literature, which dates, however, from at least half a millennium later. The pioneers of Aegean prehistory blamed the collapse on the invasion of the Dorians into southern Greece and their subjugation of local populations, which ancient tradition placed shortly after the Trojan War (see Hall 1997: 56–65, 114; Middleton 2010: 31, with references). The geographic distribution of the Doric dialect and the attestation of Dorian tribal names from the Archaic period onward were mustered in support of this interpretation. Over time, ideas about the agency of the Dorians were increasingly removed from the textual tradition and were associated – however questionably – with archaeological phenomena, including the introduction of ironworking, inhumation in cist tombs or cremation, handmade burnished ware or Protogeometric pottery, new types of swords (Naue II), and certain types of metal pins and fibulae (e.g. Skeat 1934; Mylonas 1966: 218–33; Hall 1997: 115 8; Morris 2000: 198–201; Middleton 2010: 43–4). Pictorial pottery with scenes of fighting over land and sea (Figure 2), and "warrior graves," both phenomena dated to the twelfth century (see Section 3), have also been associated with the Dorian invasion and with other interpretations of the collapse centered on violence. Over time, the homeland of the Dorians was relocated from Thessaly (which was mentioned in ancient literature) to Epirus, Macedonia, and as far as the Balkans and Central Europe, without solid reasoning (as explained, e.g., in Bulatović, Molloy & Filipović 2021). Although the idea that the Dorian invasion was a catalyst for ethnic/racial and cultural – rather than social – change persisted in the great syntheses of the early 1970s (Snodgrass 1971: 8–10, 177–9, 300–4; Desborough 1972: 322–4) and beyond (Duray 2020: 109–28,

Figure 2 Krater from Kalapodi (LH IIIC-middle) showing the besieging of a coastal city. Courtesy of Wolf-Dietrich Niemeier. Reconstruction Barbara and Wolf-Dietrich Niemeier; digitalisation Peter Baumeister.

155–62, 205–15, 225–8, with references). From the postwar period, scholars increasingly identified problems with dating this phenomenon to the time of the collapse, questioned its alleged material correlates, and, eventually, deconstructed its textual basis (esp. Hall 1997: 118–28; Dickinson 2006: 3–4, 44–5, 50–4). By that time, the case of the Dorians had been undermined by the range of alternative interpretations for the palatial collapse, which emerged from the 1960s and 1970s, often in response to contemporary concerns (O'Brien 2013). However, the idea of a northern invasion has not been eclipsed (Ruppenstein 2020).

Some of the interpretations introduced in the 1960s–1970s attributed the collapse of the Aegean palaces to the Sea Peoples, who were blamed by Egyptian sources for causing havoc in the Levant ca. 1200 BCE (Vermeule 1960; Sandars 1964; 1978: 179–95; Hooker 1976: 156–62). Although this interpretation was intended as a reaction to the case for the Dorians, the two were not always treated as mutually exclusive (e.g., Sandars 1964; Drews 1993: 48–65). Unlike the argument for the Dorians, which involved an actual invasion, that for the Sea Peoples focused on economic collapse caused by their disruption of overseas trade across the Eastern Mediterranean, which deprived the Aegean palaces of essential raw materials. In the last decades, scholars have revisited the Egyptian sources on the Sea Peoples, have criticized past attempts to identify the agency of these people in the archaeological record of the Levant, and have generated revised understandings of their history (e.g., Fischer & Bürge 2017). Arguments for the role of the Sea Peoples on the Aegean collapse remain current (e.g. Jung 2017; Cline 2021: 138–43; Knapp 2021), and include hypotheses which envisage them as mercantile agents who disrupted palatial monopolies in overseas trade (Sherratt 1998; Broodbank 2013: 468–9), or as warriors once employed by the Mycenaean palaces, who possibly contributed to their collapse, and formed bands to raid the Eastern Mediterranean (e.g. Wiener 2017: 53–5, 57; Maran 2022: 241). This perspective relates to sociological analyses that link social change to the ebb and flow of trade and globalization (Chase-Dunn & Babones 2006; Chase-Dunn & Lerro 2014).

Other scholars attributed the archaeologically documented destructions of Mycenae and Thebes ca. 1200 BCE to internal strife, inspired by mythological traditions which hold that, at around the time of the Trojan War, the royal house of Mycenae suffered from infighting, while Thebes was destroyed by an Argive army (Andronikos 1954: 237; Mylonas 1966: 226–7). Although these suggestions were brief and tentative, and did not attract support, the idea that competition and warfare between palatial polities had a detrimental impact on the Mycenaean world is gaining in popularity (e.g., Middleton 2010: 50–2; Wiener 2017: 51; Stockhammer 2024: 121–2).

Manolis Andronikos (1954: esp. 237–9) ascribed the Mycenaean collapse to peasant revolts against the ruling class. His neo-Marxist approach revamped the Dorians into the lower class of Mycenaean polities who revolted against their masters (Hooker 1976: 173, 179), and inspired the – now dismissed – identification of elements of the Doric dialect in the language of the Linear B tablets (Chadwick 1976). Although overlooked at the time (see Mylonas 1966: 231–2), this approach resurfaced in recent scholarship which holds that a social revolution, caused not by the Dorians but by the over-exploited Mycenaean populace, resulted in the looting and burning of the palaces (Jung 2017; Maran 2022: 233, 234–6; *contra* Cline 2021: 137–8).

A very different hypothesis, which also emerged in the 1960s, holds that the collapse of Greece and the Eastern Mediterranean ca. 1200 BCE was caused by an epidemic (Williams 1962). This hypothesis, however, is not grounded in any textual or other evidence from Greece itself, while any related information from elsewhere in the Eastern Mediterranean remains rare and dates from other periods (Walløe 1999; Wiener 2017: 47–8). Accordingly, the hypothesis remains unpopular (Middleton 2010: 50–2; Cline 2021: 150–2), even after the Covid-19 pandemic, which reminded humanity of the heavy toll of epidemics and their impact on social change.

Hypotheses for the effect of nonanthropogenic factors on the collapse of the Mycenaean palaces include a wave of earthquakes. Greece lies in the middle of the collision between the Eurasian and African tectonic plates, and has thus suffered perennially from earthquakes. Earthquake damage is identifiable ca. 1200 BCE at the major sites of the Argolid and – to a lesser extent – at other Greek sites especially in the Peloponnese and east Central Greece, and such damage could have caused the conflagrations that consumed the Mycenaean palaces (Betancourt 1976; Nur & Cline 2000; Middleton 2010: 38–40; Cline 2021: 136–7). However, the evidence from the Argolid is lately dissociated from seismic activity (Hinojosa-Prieto 2020) and in any case is largely present in houses rather than monumental buildings; earthquakes alone cannot explain why no Mycenaean polity recovered (Dickinson 2006: 45, 46, 50; Middleton 2010: 40–1; Jung 2017: 86–7; Wiener 2017: 46–7; Maran 2022: 231–2).

Other literature treats climate change as a catalyst for palatial collapse. Although this idea has an earlier history (Carpenter 1966), and conforms to the fascination ancient historians have for environmental catastrophes (as criticized in Horden and Purcell 2000: 298–341), it is only in the last two decades that paleoenvironmental proxy data established that, from the twelfth century onward, the climate of Greece, the Eastern Mediterranean and much of Europe became considerably drier and colder, which must have put stress on socio-economic systems (e.g. Kaniewski & Van Campo 2017; Weiberg & Finné 2018; Molloy 2023). Historical comparison is indicative of the ways in which climate change can affect the productivity of the land dramatically, thus causing drought, famine, and/or social unrest. However, most scholars remain skeptical over the interpretation of climate proxies, question the relevance of such proxies to diverse geographies and micro-climates, and distrust the quality of the associated chronological resolution (Dickinson 2006: 79–80; Middleton 2010: 36–8; 2020: 13–14; Knapp & Manning 2016; Wiener 2017: 43–6; Bintliff 2020: 9–11; Cline 2021: 152–66; Lemos 2022: 16; Molloy 2023). This discourse has encouraged environmentalists to pay more attention to the long-term impact of climate change when evaluating its impact on society, as is manifested by the *Domesticated Landscapes of the Peloponnese* project at Uppsala University (Weiberg & Finné 2018), and refine their chronologies, as evidenced by a recent study proposing a megadrought in Anatolia in 1198–1196 BCE (Manning et al. 2023).

The rejection of monocausal interpretations of the collapse dominates scholarship of the last 15 years, which typically approaches the developments that shook Greece and the Eastern Mediterranean ca. 1200 BCE as the aggregate of wide-ranging stress factors (Knapp & Manning 2016: esp. 113, 138; Wiener 2017; Cline 2021: 134–66). Recent scholarship also investigates both the sequence of events surrounding the collapse of the Mycenaean palaces (Jung & Kardamaki 2022) and the longer-term historical processes that conditioned this phenomenon (Maran 2022; Stockhammer 2024).

Since the nineteenth century, the centuries following the collapse have been called a Dark Age or another Middle Ages, the two terms designating the period as a historical interlude involving cultural demise and the loss of written records and literacy in general (Morris 2000: 87–90; Kotsonas 2016: 241–2; 2020: 79). Following Thucydides (1.2–3, 1.12), scholars took the period to be characterized by the Dorian invasion and the eastward migrations of the Ionians and Aeolians, which ancient tradition dated after the Trojan War (e.g. Skeat 1934). Populations from the Greek mainland are thought to have also sought refuge in Cyprus and the Levant, based on wide-ranging archaeological evidence which remains debated (e.g. Desborough 1964: 196–214; Ruppenstein 2020; Knapp 2021), and on ongoing projects of aDNA analysis (see especially the work of the Max Planck–Harvard Research Center for the Archaeoscience of the Ancient Mediterranean). Indeed, the migrations of the period are the focus of two current projects funded by the European Research Council: Bary Molloy's (University College Dublin) *The Fall of 1200 BC: The Role of Migration and Conflict in Social Crises at the End of the Bronze Age in Southeastern Europe*, and Naoise Mac Sweeney's (University of Vienna) *Migration and the Making of the Ancient Greek World*.

Following the discoveries at Lefkandi and other intellectual breakthroughs, scholars have challenged the notion of an isolated and impoverished Greece experiencing a Dark Age, have argued for continued or revived prosperity in the twelfth century (Rutter 1992; Thomatos 2006; Van Damme 2017), and have promoted the use of the nonpejorative term EIA for the society and culture of this period (e.g., Papadopoulos 1993; Lemos 2002; Kotsonas 2016; Lemos & Kotsonas 2020). Although the finds from Lefkandi remain exceptional, discoveries from across Greece have enriched the archaeological record of the period, thus rendering any defense of the notion of a Dark Age exceptional (Murray 2017; 2018a).

As I have argued before (Kotsonas 2011), the end of the Bronze Age and its aftermath is best approached not through the traditional catastrophic scenarios and gloomy notions of Dark Ages (Snodgrass 1971; Desborough 1972; Drews 1993), or the priorities of collapsology (Middleton 2010; 2020; Cline 2021), but through an emphasis on the resilience of different communities. This notion is increasingly pursued in scholarship on the period, ranging from synthetic works (Cline 2024) to site-specific studies (Papadopoulos & Smithson 2017: 973–84; Van Damme 2017). Some have even written of the "successful collapse" of certain Aegean regions (Wallace 2010) and of the way this galvanized technological innovation (Wallace 2021). Additionally, scholarship on Western Asia of the same period observes that the emphasis on collapse and resilience/regeneration has had a limiting effect on interpretation, and seeks different models to capture the range and complexity of the historical processes manifested at the time (Masetti-Rouault et al. 2024). In this intellectual milieu, the concept of social change, which does not carry the conceptual load of some of the abovementioned terms, can help generate more balanced understandings of the period.

3 Socio-Political Change

After the Hittite Empire, with its "Great King," collapsed ca. 1200 BCE, the rulers of the regional capital of Carchemish adopted the title "Great King," thus portraying themselves as heirs to the defunct royal dynasty (Cline 2024: 112–3, 115, 208–11). No such transfer of political power is assumed for Greece (Santini 2022), not only because we lack any epigraphic evidence from the Postpalatial Aegean comparable to the royal inscriptions from Carchemish, but also because "a ruling elite marked by really distinctive forms of tomb or building is impossible to identify" in Greece (Dickinson 2006: 74; cf. Thomatos 2006: 259).

Socio-political change across the end of the Aegean Bronze Age is traditionally captured by the model *From Wanax to Basileus* (Deger-Jalkotzy & Lemos 2006; cf. Crielaard 2011; Bettelli 2015; on these terms, see Middleton 2010: 92–4; Crielaard 2011: 83–7, with references). The model holds that, following the collapse, the *wa-na-ka* and his senior administration disappeared, while the *qa-si-re-we*, local officials of the administration, emerged as chieftains and eventually became the Homeric *basileis*, or kings (though Jung 2017: 102 hypothesizes that the *basileis* had an active role in the palatial collapse). Although the model is grounded on rich textual evidence from Linear B and the Homeric epics, it has been criticized for being linear and insensitive to regional trajectories, for telescoping what was probably a drawn-out process (Crielaard 2011), and for underestimating that authority in Homer does not lie exclusively with the *basileis* (Kõiv 2016: 296–7; Cosmopoulos 2025: 68–78). Additionally, recent research has questioned the impression that Postpalatial Greece was characterized by low socio-political complexity, and it has (re)-interpreted certain archaeological contexts to argue that the collapse offered opportunities for individuals and communities to establish new forms of authority (e.g. Van Damme 2017; Eder & Lemos 2020: 136). Interest in inequality in the Greek EIA has risen lately (Cerasuolo 2021: Chapters 8–10), but the possibility of nonhierarchical forms of social organization (Graeber & Wengrow 2021) remains unexplored.

After they were burned down, some of the Mycenaean palaces were abandoned and others attracted limited cleaning and reoccupation, but a few witnessed rebuilding (Maran & Papadimitriou 2020: 702) and others may have emerged as foci of social memory (Maran 2025). Postpalatial Tiryns presents exceptional evidence for this and for broader urban revival, which indicates the rise of new forms of political authority in the twelfth century (Maran & Papadimitriou 2006; 2020: 702–4; Mühlenbruch 2013; Maran 2016). Extensive evidence for urban revival is identifiable both on the Lower Citadel and outside it (Maran 2016; see Section 6). However, only two important areas of the Upper Citadel were cleared of debris to be reused: the ruined megaron and the Great Court before it, with the altar. A narrow (20.9 m by 6.9 m), Postpalatial structure, Building T, was constructed above the eastern part of the ruined megaron (Maran 2000; 2012). It consisted of an approximately square porch and an elongated inner room divided by a central row of columns. Incorporating the area of the throne of the Palatial megaron but showing no central hearth and no wall paintings (which were central to palatial ideology; see Section 8), Building T stood in isolation and was probably an assembly hall, which both referenced and replaced the authority of the earlier megaron (Mühlenbruch 2013: 269–73). The open space surrounding this building and the altar must have attracted rituals attended by large parts of the populace. Apparently, social groups of the Postpalatial period appropriated monuments and portable remains of the Palatial past to legitimize their positions in a volatile world, and redeployed these remains in ways which fitted the new socio-political landscape (Maran 2012; 2016: 210; Kõiv 2016: 321–2; Maran & Papadimitriou 2020: 702–3).

Symptomatic of the floruit of Tiryns and of various modes of socio-political interaction in the LH IIIC period are two pictorial kraters from the site. The first krater depicts a chariot race and a seated person who is holding a kylix and is either offering libations or participating in a feast, this imagery being probably inspired by competitive contests and rituals held at the time (Valavanis 2020). The second krater (Figure 3) shows four pairs of warriors, including one engaged in a duel, and another shaking hands, as well as a pair of fortified cities with spectators on the walls (Chatzina et al. 2023). The handshake scene, perhaps the earliest handshake in art, has been interpreted in the light of the Homeric epics as a scene of forging an alliance, and is tentatively taken to represent a historical event of the time (Chatzina et al. 2023: 34–5). The pictorial kraters from Tiryns are indicative of the important role of feasting for community (re)-building and socio-political change in the turbulent period after the collapse. Feasting itself changed considerably with the collapse, as evidenced by a comparison of the Mycenaean evidence with both Homeric descriptions (Sherratt 2004; Cosmopoulos 2025: 79–80) and the archaeological record from settlement, sanctuary, and burial contexts from the twelfth century onward (Charalambidou 2025).

The Tiryns handshake krater is symptomatic of the marked increase of pictorial pottery with warriors and fighting on land and sea in twelfth-century Greece (Thomatos 2006: 141–2, 247–9; Bettelli 2015: 133–5). Conforming to the emphasis of Mycenaean art on collective military endeavors (Olsen 2020: 297, 299), this pottery recalls the appearance of burials with weapons, or "warrior graves." Although rarely documented in the Palatial period outside

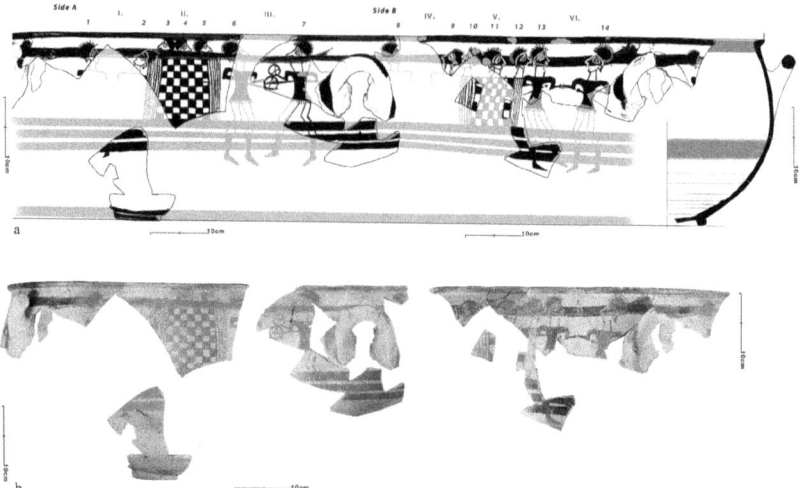

Figure 3 Tiryns Handshake Krater (LH IIIC-middle): reconstructed section and panorama view of the vessel. Drawing and photograph: M. Kostoula. After Chatzina et al. 2023. Courtesy of Joseph Maran and Alkestis Papadimitriou. Ephorate of Antiquities of the Argolid. © Hellenic Ministry of Culture – Hellenic Organisation of Cultural Resources.

Crete, in the twelfth and eleventh centuries such burials are attested in the northwestern Peloponnese (especially western Achaia), east Crete, and more sparsely in other Greek regions, especially beyond core palatial areas (Deger-Jalkotzy 2006; Giannopoulos 2007: 201–52; 2025; Middleton 2010: 101–7; Bettelli 2015: 130–6). The "warrior graves" contain a newly-introduced type of sword (Naue II), which is occasionally accompanied by spearheads and other weapons, headgears and instruments for personal adornment, including pieces imported from the Central and Eastern Mediterranean and objects showing connections with Italy, the Balkans, Crete and Cyprus (on these connections, see Moschos 2009: 371–82; Jung & Mehofer 2013; Van den Berg 2018; Di Lorenzo 2023). These burials are either cremations or inhumations and are usually deposited in chamber tombs, which can contain older burials dating to the Palatial period and/or contemporary burials that present no exquisite finds. It has been tempting to interpret the "warrior graves" (and the associated pictorial pottery) in the light of the insecurity that characterized the period. Significantly, this period has yielded palaeodemographic data for an increase in young male adult deaths that is consistent with increased violence (Moutafi 2021: 280).

The discovery of two dozen "warrior graves" in Achaia – and the rise in population and prosperity deduced for the region at the time (Giannopoulos

2007: 201–52; Moschos 2009) – were once connected to the tradition which has people from the eastern Peloponnese and their leaders fleeing there to escape the Dorians (Pausanias 7.1.7). More recent interpretations hold that Achaian "warrior graves" belong to descendants of military officers and their troops who fled the core palatial regions at the time of the collapse (Giannopoulos 2025: 13–18). Nevertheless, these interpretations find little bio-archaeological support (Moutafi 2021: 279–80) and risk inferring biographical fallacies from "warrior graves" (Whitley 2002). Most scholars hold that these tombs represent local leaders (or *basileis*) whose authority was nonhereditary and depended on their military prowess, which explains why they invested in status symbols referencing warfare, the past, and overseas connections (Dickinson 2006: 74, 243; Moschos 2009: 384; Lemos 2014: 167; Bulmer 2020: 148). This interpretation relates especially to an eleventh-century "warrior grave" from Knossos discussed below.

The eleventh century is typically considered the gloomiest part of the Dark Age, and a time of low socio-political complexity characterized by small, and more or less egalitarian communities (e.g., Morris 1997: 542; Dickinson 2006: 175, 190, 246). These notions can be questioned on both theoretical (Graeber & Wengrow 2021) and empirical grounds, the latter pertaining to the case of Knossos, as evidenced by the earliest tomb at the Knossos North Cemetery (KNC tomb 201). Established after the abandonment of various LBA cemeteries around Knossos, ca. 1 km north of the then ruined Minoan palace, the KNC was to become the largest and richest burial ground of the community for half a millennium (Coldstream & Catling 1996; also, Section 6). Tomb 201 was a pit-cave and contained the earliest cremation at the site, including the remains of a male, a female, and perhaps a child, who were accompanied by an exceptional range of bronze weapons (a sword, a spearhead, five or six arrowheads, and a shield boss) (Figure 4), in addition to an antique boar's-tusk helmet, bone inlays attributed to a quiver made of perishable material, an antique Cypriot bronze stand, an iron knife, two iron pins, a gold ring, an ivory comb, an ivory handle and bronze fragments perhaps from tweezers (Kotsonas 2018; Hatzaki & Kotsonas 2020: 1039–41). This tomb, and KNC tomb 186, "are not only the richest at present known from Knossos; they must be richer than any contemporary burials not only in SM [Subminoan] Crete but in SMyc [Submycenaean] Greece as well" (Coldstream & Catling 1996: 715).

The range of weapons in the KNC tomb 201 is exceptional for Greece of the time, and includes several rarely attested pieces (Kotsonas 2018: 21). Intriguingly, this range matches the equipment which the Cretan hero Meriones carries in *Iliad* 10.260–265, which is extraordinary for a Homeric Greek hero. Thus, the male occupant of Tomb 201 and the Iliadic persona of

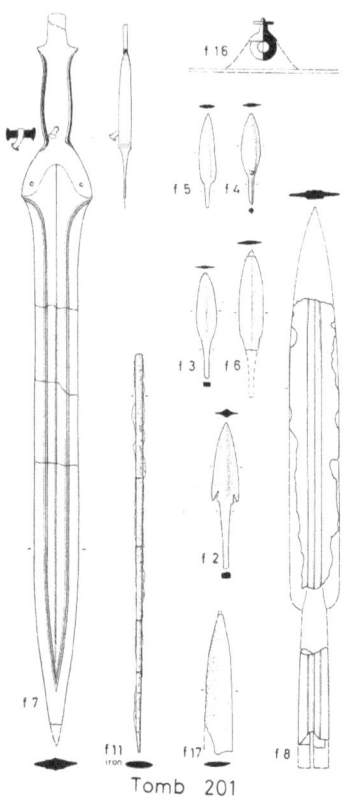

Figure 4 Weapons from the Subminoan tomb 201 of the Knossos North Cemetery. Reproduced with permission of the British School at Athens.

Meriones share (a) a Cretan and particularly Knossian identity of high status, (b) an unusually broad range of weapons, including pieces that are otherwise rare in both the epic and the archaeological record, (c) an association with antique objects, especially a boar's-tusk helmet. These correspondences recall the philological argument that Cretan stories centered on Meriones underlie different parts of the Homeric epics (Kotsonas 2018: 22–3). It is conceivable that a Cretan poet composed a work praising the military prowess and the weapons of the distinguished male occupant of KNC tomb 201 for performance on the occasion of his funeral, as Hesiod may have done for Amphidamas of Chalkis (*Works and Days* 650–60). The hypothesis that such a composition dates from the eleventh century recalls the influential argument that this phase was formative for the Homeric epics and the Greek concept of the hero (Kotsonas 2018: 24, with references). However, the same argument is compatible with the alternative hypothesis that an earlier poem about Meriones, which is hypothesized on philological grounds, could have inspired the kin of a prominent Knossian to stage his funeral as a performance that promoted the connection of the deceased with the hero (Kotsonas 2018: 25–6). In any case, tomb 201 is indicative of the performance of probably new forms of political authority at death.

A lavish double burial that inaugurated a major cemetery is also attested at Lefkandi Toumba (Catling & Lemos 1990; Popham, Calligas, & Sackett 1993; Lemos 2002: 140–5; Pierattini 2022b). This burial was found within the largest (ca. 50 m long) and most monumental structure known from anywhere in Greece between 1200 and 800 BCE. Crowning the Toumba hillock located 500 m east of the Xeropolis settlement, and dating from ca. 950 BCE, the elongated apsidal structure is made of a stone socle supporting walls made of plastered mudbrick, is divided internally into three parts, and is surrounded externally by a veranda of wooden posts, which supported a thatched roof. Stratigraphy confirms that the Toumba building was short-lived, but leaves open whether the two large rock-cut burial shafts found in it predate or postdate its construction. The excavators identified the building as a funerary monument for a distinguished community leader and his wife (and perhaps even a *heroon*, though there is no evidence for cult) (Catling & Lemos 1990; Popham, Calligas, & Sackett 1993; Lemos 2002: 145–6, 166–8), but others identify it as the abode of this leader which was turned into his burial monument (Whitley 1991b: 350; Crielaard & Driessen 1994; Mazarakis Ainian 1997: 53–7; Morris 2000: 221), both interpretations presenting gender biases (Harrell 2014. Cf. evidence from the Torone cemetery suggesting that "it was not always a male that assumed primary importance": Papadopoulos 2005: 405). The leading couple was buried in one of the two burial shafts. The cremated remains of the man were held in an antique Cypriot amphora, which represents the earliest inurned cremation at Lefkandi. The amphora, whose mouth was closed by a bronze bowl, contained an impressive garment and was accompanied by a sword, a razor, a spearhead, and a whetstone. The same shaft yielded the inhumation of a woman, who was probably placed in a wooden coffin, with hands folded and legs crossed, and was furnished with gold and other jewelry, including a Babylonian gold pendant of 1700–1600 BCE. The position of the woman's limbs and a knife found next to her head suggest she may have been ritually executed. The second shaft contained the remains of four horses, which had been sacrificed on the spot and thrown into the shaft. After the shafts were closed, a large krater was placed nearby, probably to serve as a burial marker and collect libations; then, the building was partly dismantled and buried under a tumulus which marked the site. Shortly after, the east foot of the tumulus attracted burials which were furnished with gold ornaments, Near Eastern imports, and other finds which are considerably rarer in the other cemeteries of Lefkandi and beyond. This suggests that an elite burial group, distinguished by its wealth and overseas connections, chose this location to associate itself with the exceptional couple buried in the Toumba building, who may have been instrumental in the accumulation of this wealth and the development of these connections.

Many scholars relate the Lefkandi Toumba burials to the Homeric burials of Patroclus (*Iliad* 18.336–37, 23.22–23, 23.161–257) and Achilles (*Odyssey* 24.60–84) (Popham, Calligas, & Sackett 1993; Antonaccio 1995: 15–20; Morris 2000: 235; Lemos 2002: 216–7; *contra* Kõiv 2016: 307–8). Others consider that structures like the Toumba building "could well have been the homes of real-life counterparts to the Homeric *basileis*" (Dickinson 2006: 110), and they assume that the *basileus* buried there passed his rule to an aristocracy buried in the associated cemetery (Lemos 2002: 217–20; Kõiv 2016: 302–8). Anthropological perspectives focus instead on the evidence provided by the Toumba building for the hierarchical organization of a community of the period, and the capacity of its leaders to mobilize craftsmen to build at an exceptional scale, to afford the conspicuous consumption of livestock and material wealth, and to mobilize a large community of people to bury the building under the tumulus. This level of socio-political complexity was unthinkable for the period before the discoveries at Lefkandi, and remains unique for Greece. Possible comparisons have been identified at Megaron B at Thermon in Aetolia (Morris 2000: 222–8) and at Amos on the Karian Chersonese (Gürbüzer 2022). However, the former case has been dismissed (Papapostolou 2008), and the latter is much smaller in scale and elaboration.

4 Demography and Social Change

The continuity of occupation and relative prosperity seen at Tiryns, Knossos, and Lefkandi after the collapse is rather exceptional for Greece of the time. Indeed, scholarship assumes a major wave of settlement abandonment and population decline over the two centuries which followed the collapse (Snodgrass 1971: 360–78; Desborough 1972: 18–25; Middleton 2010: 68–91). This is traditionally explained by increased mortality during these violent times, prolonged hardship, and the migration of populations from the Mycenaean palatial areas to elsewhere in Greece and the Eastern Mediterranean. This section revisits the basis for the assumed demographic drop and the associated ideas on social change.

The impression of a major population decline in Greece from the thirteenth to the eleventh century relies on the remarkable drop in site numbers, which is documented by both excavation and surface survey (Middleton 2010: 68–71; Murray 2018a: 30–41; Knodell 2021: 33–45, 119–20). In Snodgrass's estimates, the drop was as high as 92% (from ca. 320 to ca. 40 sites). Jonathan Hall's (2014: 60, figure 3.4; cf. Murray 2017: 238) more up-to-date dataset suggests a drop of ca. 62% from the thiteenth to the twelfth century, and an equal drop from the twelfth to the eleventh century. Notwithstanding these grand estimates, scholars acknowledge regional variation and agree that Crete shows an exceptionally high number of settlement sites despite the major changes seen in their size and placement after ca. 1200 BCE (Nowicki 2000; 2025; Dickinson 2006: 90–3; Wallace 2010: 52–75, 104–13, and esp. 54; Pollard 2023; also, Section 6 below).

Based on the sharp drop in site numbers, Desborough (1972: 18) hypothesized that, from 1200 to 1100 BCE, Greece lost 90% of its population, while Snodgrass (1971: 367) argued for a drop of over 75% from 1200 to 1000 BCE. More recently, Morris (2007: 218) and Murray (2017: 211, 237) proposed softer declines of 50–75% and 40–60%, respectively. The above establishes that, over the last half-century, estimates for a drop in settlement have decreased by 30%, and estimates for population decline have decreased by as much as 50%. Revisions in absolute chronology (see Appendix) may lead to further decrease.

Remarkable population decline is also indicated by guesstimates over site size and extrapolations of population figures based on assumed occupation per hectare (for critical reflections, see e.g. Murray 2017: 214–6; Bintliff 2020: 11–24; Lemos 2022: 17). Working along these lines, John Bintliff estimated that the population of Mycenaean urban sites in the Argolid ranged from 600 to 3600, while Mycenae was exceptional in reaching 6,000 (Bintliff 2020: 21, Table 1.1.1). Such population levels re-emerged in Greece only in the eighth century (Hall 2014: 75, fig. 4.1). In the period around 1000 BCE, most sites were inhabited by 100–200 people (e.g. Wallace 2010: 62; Hall 2014: 61; Kotsonas 2021: 66), and only a few could have reached 4-digit population figures (Hall 2014: 61 for Argos; Kotsonas 2021: 66–7, for Knossos and Karphi; Pollard & Whitelaw 2025, Table 2, for Knossos).

In the last quarter century, scholars increasingly argue that the impression of a major population decline across the end of the Bronze Age may be exaggerated by problems of archaeological visibility and methodological flaws in data collection, classification, and interpretation (Dickinson 2006: 93–8; Middleton 2010: 70–1; Stissi 2011; Murray 2017: 214–30; 2018a: 30–41; Bintliff 2020: 12; Lemos 2022: 17–18). Indeed, the survival and visibility of the settlement record of the period is affected disproportionately by the form of the houses (largely made of perishable materials such as timber, mudbrick and thatch), the main settlement pattern (dispersed, with clusters of houses separated by large open spaces), and the location of sites and associated site formation processes (on hilltops heavily affected by erosion and/or on places occupied for long periods). Conversely, the higher visibility of Cretan Postpalatial settlements depends partly on their distinct topography, which has saved them from overbuilding and alluviation. Additional problems of visibility pertain to the ceramic record of the period, which is characterized by a relatively high percentage of plain and coarse ware and a paucity of type-fossils, thus presenting lower rates of survival and diagnosticity. Such considerations have led some to question the assumed population decline, and to attribute the pattern of site abandonment to the centralization of population in fewer sites (e.g., Tiryns) or to the dispersal of people across the countryside; however, these ideas remain unsupported (Dickinson 2006: 84–8, 93–4; Murray 2017: 232–3).

An ingenious explanation for the lower visibility of settlements in EIA Greece came from Snodgrass (1971: 380; 1980a: 35–6; and esp. 1987: 189–210), who argued that Greeks of the period turned to nomadic pastoralism involving transhumance and the seasonal occupation of sites, which leaves only a small footprint in the archaeological record. Snodgrass's argument was based on a range of evidence, including the short life of many settlements of the period, the popularity of apsidal houses which ethnoarchaeology associates with pastoralists (cf. Jazwa 2019: 163–4), the prominence of cattle in Homer, the widespread attestation of votive figurines of cattle in EIA sanctuaries (Figure 5), and the unusual abundance of cattle bone at EIA layers at Nichoria (the first site of the period to attract a zooarchaeological analysis), which contrasted with the record from the LBA layers (Sloan & Duncan 1978).

Figure 5 Bronze cattle of the EIA from the Cretan sanctuary of Agia Triada. Archaeological Museum of Heraklion. © Hellenic Ministry of Culture – Hellenic Organisation of Cultural Resources.

Scholars have criticized the theoretical underpinnings of Snodgrass's hypothesis, and the reliability of the different strands of evidence mustered to support it (Cherry 1988: 27–30; Palmer 2001: 67–71; Dickinson 2006: 98–104). Also, they have argued that Greece of the period presents numerous sedentary communities, and they have observed that the sites which have since attracted zooarchaeological and archaeobotanical analyses do not show the economic emphasis on cattle observed at Nichoria (e.g. Thomas & Conant 1999: 43–6; Whitley 2001: 85–6; Dickinson 2006: 101–3; Hall 2014: 62; Dibble & Finné 2021). Additional problems for the pastoralist hypothesis emerge from recent scientific analyses. Indeed, a diachronic review of nitrogen isotope ratios from Greek burials found that animal protein consumption dropped markedly in the EIA (Papathanasiou & Richards 2015). Additionally, a reanalysis of the bone assemblage from Nichoria demonstrated that the increase of cattle observed at the EIA levels of the site was due to postdepositional taphonomy: due to their location in the soil column, the animal bones of the EIA levels were more weathered than those of the lower-lying LBA levels, and cattle bone survived better than the bone of smaller species, thus skewing the recovered dataset (Dibble & Fallu 2020). When EIA bone assemblages from the site are well-preserved, they do not show any increased presence of cattle. This discourse has been fundamental for our understanding of society, economy, and settlement in this period, and is revisited in the next two sections.

All in all, it remains hard to deny that the number and size of settlements declined markedly after 1200 BCE; however, the dramatic impression conveyed in previous scholarship is demonstrably exaggerated, and relevant estimates were shown to have dropped by 30% to 50% over the last half century, with major implications for our understanding of the scale and pace of social change.

5 Socio-Economic Change, and Exchange

For a long time, the economy of the Aegean Bronze Age was juxtaposed with that of the EIA. This notion was promoted especially by Moses Finley (e.g. Finley 1956; 1957) and Colin Renfrew (1972: 296–7, 464; also, Palmer 2001: 43–50; Killen 2008), who thought that the Mycenaean palaces (like their Near Eastern counterparts) were the centers of regional redistributive economic systems (while also engaging in reciprocal exchange with major polities elsewhere in the Eastern Mediterranean). Over time, the palaces developed overspecialized economies through, for example, monocultural production on large estates, which made them vulnerable to collapse. This economic regime was contrasted to the one which emerged after the collapse, which was based on small-scale mixed farming and gift-exchange between leaders, as deduced from the Homeric epics; market exchange was taken to emerge only in the eighth century, as inferred from Hesiod's *Works and Days* (this text-based and linear model was canonized as *Warriors into Traders* in Tandy 1997). Other scholars elaborated on the assumed contrast between the LBA and EIA economies. For example, Snodgrass juxtaposed the mixed agropastoral economic regime of the Palatial period with the pastoral economy of the EIA (see above). Broadening the geographic and thematic scope of the comparison, others envisaged state-sponsored, institutional economies around the LBA Eastern Mediterranean engaged in reciprocal relationships, and contrasted them to the private entrepreneurship of the EIA (Sherratt & Sherratt 1992–3; Sherratt 1998).

In the last two decades, the perceived polarity of the economies across the end of the Bronze Age has been eroded. Indeed, scholarship has shown that the extent of the palatial grip over the Mycenaean economy was not as extensive as previously thought, and has identified economic activities lying outside state control (Halstead 1992; Foxhall 1995; Bennet 2007: 190–1, 195–6; Galaty & Parkinson 2007; Pratt 2025: 25–51). To Paul Halstead, the palace administration recorded the bulk production of wheat, wool and olive oil, but it did not capture the mixed economies of secondary and small sites that covered a range of crops and livestock; sometimes, the palaces did not own the land or the flocks which produced the goods, but partnered with local communities or private individuals (Halstead 1999; 2001; cf. Killen 1998; Palmer 2001: 155–64; Lupack 2011; Zurbach 2017: 33–217; Pratt 2021: 99–111). Thus, the emerging consensus is that the Mycenaean elite households had an entrepreneurial and highly involved role in the economic and administrative activities of the state (cf. Bennet 2007: 194–5; Murray 2017: 247–54; Nakassis 2020: 272–4, 281–2; 2025; Pratt 2021: 178). This approach assumes "substantial continuity in economic units and strategies across the LBA and EIA and suggests economic changes be understood in relational, rather than typological, terms" (Nakassis 2020: 272; cf. Foxhall 1995; Zurbach 2017).

The novel understanding of the Mycenaean economy also encompasses the modes of Mycenaean craft production, which are found to lie along a continuum: from household production independent of any palatial control, to partial oversight or actual monopoly (Bennet 2007: 195–200; Nakassis 2020: 278). Judging by the better explored sites, palatial centers hosted the production of some high-value goods, while other workshops were situated in secondary sites and outside urban centers (Dakouri-Hild 2005: 218–9).

The production of perfumed oil and carved ivory was directly managed by palatial authorities (Killen 2001; Pratt 2025: 41–3). Different economic strategies are identifiable for textile production and the monitoring of textile workers and their output, which preoccupy more than half of known Linear B tablets (Nosch 2000; Bennet 2007: 196–200; Pratt 2025: 39–41). In Messenia, textile production was centralized to Pylos and very few other major sites, but the palace of Knossos controlled textile workers scattered across central Crete (Bennet 2007: 196–7; Pratt 2025: 40–1). The system of *ta-ra-si-ja*, which was used for the production of metal objects, some kinds of textiles, and other goods, had the palaces allocate raw materials to producers at various locations, with the expectation of finished products in return (Killen 2001; Bennet 2007: 198). The numerous hoards of both complete and broken bronze tools dating from ca. 1200 BCE may be remnants of this system (Blackwell 2018). Pottery production may have been handled differently by different polities. At Mycenae, fineware pottery production for export came under the control of – or at least within the orbit of – the palatial authority (Parkinson & Pullen 2014: 77–8), while the production site of Kontopigado in Attica was probably controlled by the authority on the Athenian Acropolis (Day & Kardamaki 2025: 146–51). At Pylos, a single potter designated as "royal" provided most of the pottery found in the palace; however, this pottery is not of export quality, and the different communities of the Pylian state must have been served by local potters operating outside palatial control (Bennet 2007: 1978; Day & Kardamaki 2025: 143).

The Linear B tablets do not contain direct information on economic exchange between the Mycenaeans and the Eastern Mediterranean, but wide-ranging exchange is indicated by archaeology (Cline 1994; Murray 2017: 32–46, 73–85, 112–29; 2023b). The Uluburun wreck of a ship which was probably heading to the Aegean loaded with ten tons of Cypriot copper and one ton of tin (in addition to other goods), in the late fourteenth century, is commonly associated with the kinds of kingly exchanges mentioned in the letters from Amarna, Egypt; this evidence is fundamental to the idea that state-sponsored enterprises dominated the Eastern Mediterranean economies of the LBA (Sherratt & Sherratt 1992–3; Sherratt 1998; Bennet 2007: 202–3; with skepticism in Murray 2023a: 34–5). However, other shipwrecks with smaller and different cargos – for example, the Cape Gelidonya wreck, which carried one ton of bronze in ingots but also scrap, or the Point Iria wreck, which only held pottery – may be indicative of independent traders (Dickinson 2006: 34–5; Bennet 2007: 203; Nakassis 2020: 281–2). Mycenaean pottery – from finewares which circulated empty to coarse stirrup-jars and other containers of foodstuffs and (perfumed) oil – and perhaps perishable goods (such as textiles) were exported from the Aegean to the Eastern Mediterranean (Cline 1994; Broodbank 2013: 373–415; Murray 2017: 124–7, 192–9; 2023a: 36–40; 2023b; Sherratt 2020: 191–4; Pratt 2021: 132–47; Graziadio 2025: 351–97). Judging by Cypro-Minoan marks and other evidence, Mycenaean pottery was exported to the

Eastern Mediterranean in Cypriot hands (Sherratt 2020: 193; Murray 2023a: 35–6).

Greek and Eastern Mediterranean economies suffered heavily from the collapse of 1200 BCE. After this point, no powerful economic institutions are identifiable in Greece. The Homeric epics sketch an economy centered on the *oikos* and its self-sufficiency, with gift exchange practiced between the heads of powerful households, which has informed generalized understandings of the Greek EIA economy (Finley 1956; Nakassis 2020: 277, 285–6; Lemos 2022: 19–23, 27; Pratt 2025: 55–6). Households may have held important economic roles in the LBA (Nakassis 2025), but these roles were revamped in the very different Postpalatial economic framework. An emphasis on self-sufficiency can be deduced from the increased investment in household storage in Postpalatial times (Thomatos 2006: 213–4; Van Damme 2017: 361–87; Pratt 2021: 160–2; 2025: 55–6; Lemos 2022: 20–1). This investment can be interpreted as a response to the disappearance of the palatial storage facilities and the long-distance mechanisms of exchange of the LBA; it is unlikely to represent any increased emphasis on agricultural production, since pollen evidence shows a decrease in human pressure on the landscape (Weiberg et al. 2019: 754). Archaeobotanical and pollen evidence confirms that the types of agricultural produce of the Palatial era – different species of cereal (especially barley and – to a lesser extent – wheat), legumes, and fruit (especially olives, grapes, and figs) – largely continued to be cultivated after the collapse (Megaloudi 2006: 77–9; Pratt 2021: 158–60, 201–3; 2025; 52–4). Agricultural strategies are also likely to have remained stable, especially in areas that fell outside the palatial orbit (Diffey et al. 2025).

The intensified attention given to archaeobotanical and zooarchaeological remains is one of the factors which has put to rest the pastoralist hypothesis of Snodgrass (1971: 380; 1980a: 35–6; and esp. 1987: 189–10; see Section 4). New faunal analyses indicate that the relatively homogenous system of animal husbandry that is identifiable in Mycenaean times, probably due to palatial control, was succeeded by heterogeneous systems in the EIA (Dibble & Finné 2021). Accordingly, in areas with less rainfall, the LBA emphasis on sheep was succeeded by an EIA emphasis on goats, which may have been an adaptive response to the drier climate. Postpalatial regionalism is also indicated by the considerable differences between faunal assemblages from the Peloponnese and Central Greece (Van Damme 2017: 382–7). Additionally, analytical studies show that the EIA is characterized by a marked drop in the consumption of meat (Papathanasiou and Richards 2015: 198, 201) and suggest the movement of animals between the Aegean and other Mediterranean regions before and after the collapse (Meiri et al. 2019).

The collapse of the Mycenaean palaces came along with the breakdown of the institutional supply of raw materials, a serious demise in the demand for numerous classes of finished goods, and a loss of specialized workers. Accordingly, the archaeological record for craftsmanship in the twelfth to tenth centuries pales in comparison to that of the Palatial period, which has lent indirect support to the traditional notion of a Dark Age. Some types of Mycenaean craftsmanship (e.g. monumental building, wall-painting, ivory working) disappeared, others persisted with a notable drop in the scale – but not necessarily the skill – of production (textiles, perfumed oils, pottery) (Dickinson 2006: 72–3, 114–21; Nakassis 2020: 278–9; Pratt 2025: 54–5; see also Lemos & Kotsonas 2020: Section III). Nevertheless, complex and costly products of craftsmanship, such as the chariot and the oared galley, survived the collapse (Dickinson 2006: 247; Eder & Lemos 2020: 137; Nakassis 2020: 279–80). The following overview of craftsmanship begins with metals (especially the shift from bronze to iron), and continues with other classes of material.

The Aegean is not rich in copper ores (except for Lavrion), and in the Palatial period, much copper was imported from Cyprus, with tin coming from further east (Murray 2023a: 36–7). The collapse of the palaces and overseas trade ca. 1200 BCE led to a (considerably more) decentralized model of acquiring and processing copper and tin, a reduced repertory of objects, and a relatively sparser representation of these objects in the archaeological record (Dickinson 2006: 150–71; Murray 2017: 165–82; Pratt 2025: 54–5). For example, the broad repertory of Mycenaean bronze vessels (which was reduced significantly already in the thirteenth century) reached a nadir in the eleventh century; however, from the tenth century it expanded considerably to encompass a variety of new vessel forms (Matthäus & Vonhoff 2020). Characteristic of the period surrounding the collapse is the high number of bronze hoards, which have been variously taken to reflect the insecurity of the period, a new desire to control wealth by removing it from circulation, or the introduction of Italian ritual practices (Borgna 2024: 9–11; *contra* Blackwell 2018). Indeed, the Italian- and Central European-type or provenance of numerous bronzes in these hoards is indicative of mobility between Italy and Greece in the twelfth century (Jung & Mehofer 2013; Van den Berg 2018; Di Lorenzo 2023). New exchange networks are also indicated by chemical analyses of bronzes from the Aegean, which establish that, from at least the mid-tenth century, copper was imported from the ores at Wadi Arabah in southern Israel, probably through Phoenician and Cypriot intermediaries (Kiderlen et al. 2016). Despite the more diversified sources of copper and finished bronzes imported to the Aegean in the early 1st millennium, Cyprus retains a key role (Kassianidou 2023: 337–8; Graziadio 2025: 332–3). Indeed, both before and especially after the collapse, a range of bronze vessels of different shapes were imported from Cyprus, including tripods and stands which inspired the production of Aegean counterparts (Matthäus & Vonhoff 2020: 477, 480, 482–3, 484–5, 487).

The shift from bronze to iron is a major innovation of the postcollapse period. Iron ores occur in different parts of the Aegean, but the beginning of their exploitation remains obscure (Dickinson 2006: 83), and the few iron artifacts known from the Aegean Bronze Age are probably made of meteoritic iron (Pare 2025: 70–5). The reasons for the shift to ironworking and the origins of the new technology are debated. Early scholarship held that the introduction of ironworking revolutionized ancient economy and society (Knodell 2021: 171, with references). Also, ironworking was taken to have been monopolized by the Hittite empire and to have spread with its collapse (*contra* Waldbaum 1978: 21; Lemos 2002: 101–2), though recent studies emphasize the speed with which the iron industry was established on Cyprus and iron objects became accessible to wider segments of its population (Palermo 2023; Pare 2025: 55–69). The introduction of this technology to the Aegean was once associated with the Dorian invasion (Hall 1997: 115, with references), but in the last half century it is regarded as a gradual socio-economic process, even if scholars debate the evidential and methodological basis for this deduction (Snodgrass 1971: 228–31; 1980b; Waldbaum 1978; Lemos 2002: 101; Pare 2025: 70–112). According to Snodgrass's (1971: 237–49) "bronze-shortage hypothesis," the interruption in the supply of copper and especially tin, caused by the breakdown in seafaring across the Eastern Mediterranean, led to the development of iron technology in the "more advanced" regions of the Aegean, and to the recycling of older objects in peripheral areas. However, this hypothesis is unlikely for several reasons (Morris 2000: 208–18; Dickinson 2006: 144–50; Murray 2017: 174–7, 261–3; 2023a: 44–5; Van Damme 2017: 407–8; Knodell 2021; 171–6). The marked variation in tin content seen in bronzes from Greek EIA contexts is ascribed to the use of new alloys, rather than the melting down of earlier objects. Additionally, the narrow range and rare attestations of iron objects in Greece of the late 2nd millennium (largely knives and rings) is not indicative of a shift from bronze to iron, and does not compare to the wide-ranging evidence for iron production and consumption in Cyprus of the same period; indeed, contextual (burial) and textual (Homeric) evidence suggests that iron was a prestige material in Greece of the time, with ironworking only taking off from around 1000 BCE (Pare 2025: 75–112). This model, however, remains to be confirmed by studies of regional trajectories in ironworking (Mokrišová & Verčík 2022, for Ionia; Pare 2025: 98).

Gold and silver are uncommon in the Aegean of the twelfth to tenth centuries, especially outside Crete (Dickinson 2006: 120, 168), and they are represented by small objects of personal adornment. Gold deposits are rare in the Aegean, and the source of gold objects of this period remains uncertain (Lemos 2022: 134). The gold finds from the Postpalatial period suggest a decline in both quantity and quality, which is the culmination of a negative trend that is traced back to Mycenaean Palatial times (Coldstream 1968: 19, 70, 311; Desborough 1972: 313–4; Konstantinidi-Syvridi 2020: 607–10). It was once thought that sophisticated techniques of gold-working were lost for several centuries after the collapse and were reintroduced by foreign craftsmen. This model remains possible, but the circulation of earlier or imported jewelry could have inspired Greek craftsmen to re-develop some of these techniques (Lemos 2002: 132–4; Konstantinidi-Syvridi 2020: 609–10, 619).

Silver ores are available in different parts of the Aegean (Vaxevanopoulos et al. 2022). Although facilities for the extraction of silver by the process of cupellation are known from Argos and Thorikos, and date to the late eleventh century and 900 BCE respectively (Coldstream 1968: 19, 70, 311; Desborough 1972: 313–4), both archaeological and textual evidence demonstrates that silver remained rare in the LBA and EIA Aegean (Sherratt 2023: 58–60). Despite this, Sherratt (2023: 60–2) hypothesizes that the quest for silver brought the Phoenicians to the Aegean, and specifically Lefkandi, at the turn of the millennium. Analysis of objects from the southern Levant undermines this model by showing that Aegean silver largely disappeared from the region with the collapse of 1200 BCE, and was replaced by Anatolian silver (Eshel et al. 2021).

Overall, the representation of metals in the Aegean of the twelfth to tenth centuries hints at reduced and/or irregular contacts within the region, and between this region and the Eastern Mediterranean, at reduced craftsmanship, and at remarkable technological and social change. Despite – or because of – their relative paucity, metals probably became "the single most significant indicators of wealth and social status" (Dickinson 2006: 121), especially given that other precious materials, such as ivory and faience, are not attested at the time. Symptomatic of this is Homer's treatment of metal objects as both prestigious and essential means to store capital (Cosmopoulos 2025: 183–6).

The Mycenaean large-scale and centralized mode of textile production disappeared with the collapse, but household production persisted and was reorganized (Van Damme 2017: 391–403); quality need not have dropped, and new tools, including cylindrical spindle whorls and spool-shaped loomweights, were introduced. Once taken as symptoms of production simplification, these tools are lately treated as symptoms of technological innovation (Wallace 2021: 399–405; Bowers 2025). The concentration of Postpalatial textile tools on coastal sites has been interpreted as evidence for export trade in textiles. The role of women in textile production in the EIA is indicated by the wear which is widely attested on the teeth of female burials from the Athenian Agora (Liston in Papadopoulos & Smithson 2017: 525–6).

It has been argued that, after 1200 BCE, pottery production was practiced at the household level and shifted from male to female hands (Dickinson 2006: 116; Murray, Chorghay & MacPherson 2020: 218–22). According to this view, the collapse of the palaces generated reduced demand for – and output and export of – pottery (especially wheelmade decorated wares), and led to despecialization and small-scale, seasonal, and localized production of simpler and often handmade wares. These possibilities are interesting, albeit questionable. The evidence for a potters' quarter at the Athenian Agora beginning from the end of the 2nd millennium (Papadopoulos 2003) was once considered exceptional and thus unrepresentative (Dickinson 2006: 118). However, a cluster of four Protogeometric kilns at Piraeus suggests otherwise (Mazarakos et al. 2008: 155), while also undermining the idea (of Papadopoulos 2003) that the potter's quarter at the Agora accounts for the totality of wheelmade painted pottery from EIA Attica. Equally questionable is the argument for a shift in gender roles in ceramic production after ca. 1200 BCE, since it relies on universalizing ethnographic comparison, rather than on empirical observation of morphological properties, as in Langdon 2015. Lastly, estimates over the scale of production may have to be revised extensively depending on current discussions over absolute chronology (see Appendix).

The collapse of 1200 BCE disrupted trade and exchange within and beyond the Aegean. Within the Aegean, Desborough (1964: 228) proposed that, following the demise of the material *koine* of the Palatial period, coastlands and islands of the central and southern Aegean developed a *koine* in pottery, metalwork, and burial during LH IIIC. The definition of the *koine* has caused considerable skepticism (Thomatos 2006: 145–8, with references), but it remains with us, and Penelope Mountjoy (2009) has proposed a ceramic "east mainland—Aegean koine" in the LH IIIC-late period. These *koinai* suggest an exchange of ideas and morphological and technological styles, but it is unclear if they had any economic or sociopolitical significance, as Irene Lemos (2002: 215) hypothesized. Regional exchange is also indicated by the circulation of pottery of the White Ware, which was probably produced in East Attica and was exported across the Central Aegean (Lis, Mommsen, & Sterba 2023).

Connections between the Aegean and the Mediterranean changed markedly in the Postpalatial period. Mycenaean exports to the Eastern Mediterranean disappeared (Murray 2017: 199–201), but local imitations of Mycenaean pottery (Mountjoy 2018), from fine painted material to cooking ware, increased remarkably in different parts of the region, which has fueled debates over the migration of Aegean populations (Sherratt 2013; Welton et al. 2019; Knapp 2021). In turn, Eastern Mediterranean imports to the Aegean decreased considerably (Murray 2017: 85–91, 112–29, 254–9). These patterns are agreed to reflect reduced and restructured long-distance seafaring, but Sarah Murray (2017: 210–46) associates them with depopulation in Greece (see Section 4). Only a few Aegean sites show considerable concentrations of imports, including the settlement of Tiryns and the cemetery of Perati. At Tiryns, twelfth-century levels show a range of Cypriot imports, while Cypriot, Egyptian, and Levantine small objects are found in various tombs at Perati, which suggests a nonexclusive access to such objects (Iakovidis 1969–70; Murray 2018b). Rhodes and Crete also show wide-ranging – even if proportionally reduced – connections in this period (Murray 2017: 91; Eder & Lemos 2020: 138), probably served by Cypriot traders (Kourou 2015: 216). Despite the demise of Aegean connections with the Eastern Mediterranean, metallurgical and other exchanges with Italy intensified remarkably in the twelfth century, as explained above.

Traditionally, the eleventh century is considered the climax of isolation and economic stagnation for the Aegean (Desborough 1964: 230–7; 1972: 29–129; Snodgrass 1971; 368–73). Yet, drawing inspiration from Desborough (1952; 127; 1972: 343), Lemos (2002: 212–21) argued that late in this century a Protogeometric *koine* encompassing different classes of material emerged over the Euboean Gulf, Thessaly, some of the Cyclades, and the Chalkidike, which she ascribed to both economic and cultural networks. Others have questioned the empirical basis for – and historical interpretations of – this *koine* (Papadopoulos 2005: 126–9; Donnellan 2017), but the wide-ranging circulation of Euboean and Attic pottery styles and actual vessels within and beyond the Aegean is undeniable from the tenth century (Lemos 2002: 27–93, 228–9; Kourou 2015; 2019; Gimatzidis 2024). More reliable evidence for socio-economic change is provided by the reappearance of Aegean standardized bulk transport containers in the late eleventh century. The earliest type is a neck-handled amphora, which is characterized by concentric circles on the shoulder and handles with a mid-rib. Once thought to have been produced in Locris, coastal Thessaly, the Thermaic Gulf, and Troy (Catling 1998; Pratt 2021: 224–30), these vessels were localized by recent chemical analysis to the Thermaic Gulf, including the western Chalkidike (Gimatzidis 2024: Chapters 3 and 6). These results largely reaffirm the better resolution of petrographic data from later specimens, which link the fabrics of the amphoras with the geology of the Thermaic Gulf, thus lending support to the proposal for naming these vessels Thermaic amphoras (Kotsonas 2012: 154–9). I have argued against the previously dominant assumption that the production and circulation of these amphoras was in Euboean hands, and in favor of their appreciation as a remarkable local economic initiative which stretched overseas (Kotsonas 2012: 159–61, 232–5). Different networks of exchange are identifiable in metalwork, with Cretan bronzeworking having a formative impact on the production of figurines and tripods in Euboea and the Greek mainland from the tenth century onward (Kotsonas 2009: 1053–4, 1057; for the figurines see also Lebessi 2002: 64–5, 251–5; Lemos 2006).

Tamar Hodos (2020) has traced the beginning of a process of Mediterranean globalization ca. 1100 BCE, thus connecting Aegean and Mediterranean archaeology with sociological approaches to globalization and social change (Chase-Dunn & Babones 2006; Chase-Dunn & Lerro 2014). However, the eleventh century record of interregional exchange is very thin: only individual Greek pots are known from the Levant, and very few Phoenician pots and small objects are attested in the eleventh century Aegean (Kourou 2015: 216–9; Murray 2017: 94–103, 112–29, 201–2, 259–65; Bourogiannis 2018; Sherratt 2020: 197–9). Major developments toward globalization or, better, the integration of Mediterranean networks are evident only from the late tenth and ninth centuries, when the scale and complexity of these contacts increased markedly, as shown, for example, by the range of Phoenician transport stirrup jars from Kommos Temple A in Crete, which are lately downdated to the ninth century (Gilboa, Waiman-Barak, & Jones 2015), and especially by the finds of Phoenician, Cypriot, Greek, Villanovan, Sardinian and other imports from Well 20017 at Utica in North Africa (López Castro et al. 2024, esp. 378–82), and from Huelva, on the Atlantic coast of Spain, the earliest of which date back to the late tenth century (Gonzáles de Canales, Llompart & Montaño 2024: esp. 344–5, which, however, does not address the argument of Gilboa, Sharon & Boaretto 2008 for downdating the earliest Phoenician pieces to the ninth century). The development of such long-distance contacts was a catalyst for social change across the Mediterranean (Hodos 2020).

Current scholarship generally credits the Phoenicians with restoring exchange networks between Greece and the Near East and developing new networks extending to the Central and Western Mediterranean (e.g., Hodos 2020: 66–94; Sherratt 2020: 199–200). This comes after decades of Hellenocentric approaches, which emphasized the agency of the Euboeans, and led to a heated discourse over the primacy of the Euboeans or the Phoenicians in restoring Mediterranean connections (Papadopoulos 1997; 2011; Dickinson 2006: 210–5; Kotsonas 2012: 233–4). Despite its merits, this discourse has fallen short of its postcolonial inspiration in failing to investigate the agency of other populations in Mediterranean interaction beyond the local scale of analysis (Kotsonas 2023: 238–9). Indeed, the new orthodoxy on

Phoenician primacy occasionally harks back to diffusionist ideas, as is illustrated, for example, by the titles of major museum exhibitions, including *From Sidon to Huelva* (Stampolidis 2003) or *Assyria to Iberia* (Aruz, Rakic, & Graff 2014) (Kotsonas 2020: 88; 2023: 238–41).

6 Settlements and Social Change

The study of settlement development across the end of the Bronze Age remains trapped in polarities and linear models. Particularly suggestive are titles like *Palace to Polis* (Lemos 2005), *Citadel to City-State* (Thomas & Conant 1999), and *Des petits habitats de l'époque mycénienne à la cité-état d'époque historique* (Kourou 2003). Settlement development within the EIA is conceptualized in comparable terms: *From Pasture to Polis* (Langdon 1993, which hints at Snodgrass's pastoralist hypothesis discussed in Section 4), *From Huts to Houses* (Mazarakis Ainian 2001), and "from curvilinear to rectangular" houses (or vice versa; see Gounaris 2007: 108). Additionally, the study of settlement – and other – remains of the EIA often shows a teleological preoccupation with the origins of the polis (e.g., Gounaris 2002; Rönnberg 2021; *contra* Papadopoulos 1993: 194–6), but is increasingly developing more nuanced approaches to settlement and social change.

The settlement record of the LBA is much better understood than that of the EIA (see, e.g., Morris 2007: 227, table 8.2), which is partly because of the paucity of final publications on EIA settlements (exceptions include Kastanas, Kavousi, Lefkandi, Nichoria, and Tiryns, see: Popham, Sackett, & Themelis 1980; McDonald, Coulson & Rosser 1983; Jung 2002; Mühlenbruch 2013; Preston Day et al. 2016). In Mycenaean Greece, site hierarchy is clearly identifiable (Bintliff 2020: 16–23), and the architecture reflects the hierarchical social structure (Tournavitou 2023). The palaces of Mycenae, Tiryns, and Pylos are distinguished by the central tripartite suite of rooms of the megaron, which follows a standard layout (with a porch, an antechamber, and a main room supplied with a large hearth and a throne) and dimensions (ca. 25 m x 13 m) (Thaler 2020: 378–82). The axiality of the megara and their decorative elaboration reinforce the unity of the complex. Variation characterizes the size of the megaron courts and other aspects of the layout of the Mycenaean palaces. A workforce of perhaps over 30 builders employed by the palace of Pylos could have engaged in state-sponsored projects of infrastructural engineering (Thaler 2020: 398–9), but the involvement of the state in urban planning is uncertain: palatial sites like Dimini or Iklaina present clearly delineated streets in central parts of the settlements, but public architecture (excluding fortifications) is rarely attested in Mycenaean towns, which also lack large open spaces

(Thaler 2020: 390). The harbor town of Korfos Kalamianos partly conforms to a grid and is taken to represent a development project sponsored by Mycenae (Pullen 2022). The annular settlement layouts, with both radial and concentric streets, seen at a few nonpalatial Mycenaean towns (Chalandritsa, Malthi, Argos) (Thaler 2020: 390–1) could represent the organic growth of hilltop settlements, but must have involved some central or communal overall planning, as is later attested for the Archaic polis (?) of Azoria in east Crete (Haggis 2013b).

Mycenaean urban sites were densely built up and had designated extra-urban funerary areas (Mycenae is exceptional in showing clusters of residences separated by open spaces and burials in the area outside the citadel) (Thaler 2020: 389). Private houses do not present palatial architectural attributes, which may be indicative of restrictions imposed by ruling groups (Tournavitou 2023). Elite residences outside the citadel of Mycenae and within the Lower Town of Tiryns are spacious, two- or multi-storied buildings characterized by a central corridor that provides access to rooms which flank it (Thaler 2020: 389). Wall paintings and Linear B tablets found within these corridor houses suggest the close association of their residents with the palatial administration. Such finds are missing from less elaborate residences of Mycenaean palatial and nonpalatial towns, which, however, can be multi-roomed and two-storied.

Unlike the settlement patterns of the Mycenaean or the Classical period, those of the EIA do not present any pronounced hierarchy (Whitley 1991b: 346), perhaps except for large sites like Knossos. Settlements of the EIA are characterized by considerably smaller buildings (Jazwa 2019: 161), which show no marked differentiation in size and elaboration (Dickinson 2006: 110; Wallace 2010: 114–6). Any buildings which stand out in size, elaboration, and find record have been identified as rulers' dwellings (Mazarakis Ainian 1997), with such deductions involving various degrees of confidence and being prone to circular reasoning. Given the remarkable discrepancies seen on the settlement record of the mainland and Crete in this period, the two are discussed separately below.

On the mainland, most settlements in palatial regions suffered sitewide destruction or shrank in LH IIIC (Thomatos 2006: 179–218; Van Damme 2017: 146–306). However, different episodes of destruction/abandonment affected distinct parts of the settlement of Eleon at different times (Lis & Van Damme 2021), whereas a few sites show expansion or prosperity. Postpalatial house size remains relatively stable, despite previous assumptions to the contrary (Van Damme 2017: 355–6).

The former palatial center of Tiryns shows both continuity and change in settlement (Figure 6; Maran & Papadimitriou 2006; 2020: 702–4; Lemos,

Social Change across the End of the Aegean Bronze Age 31

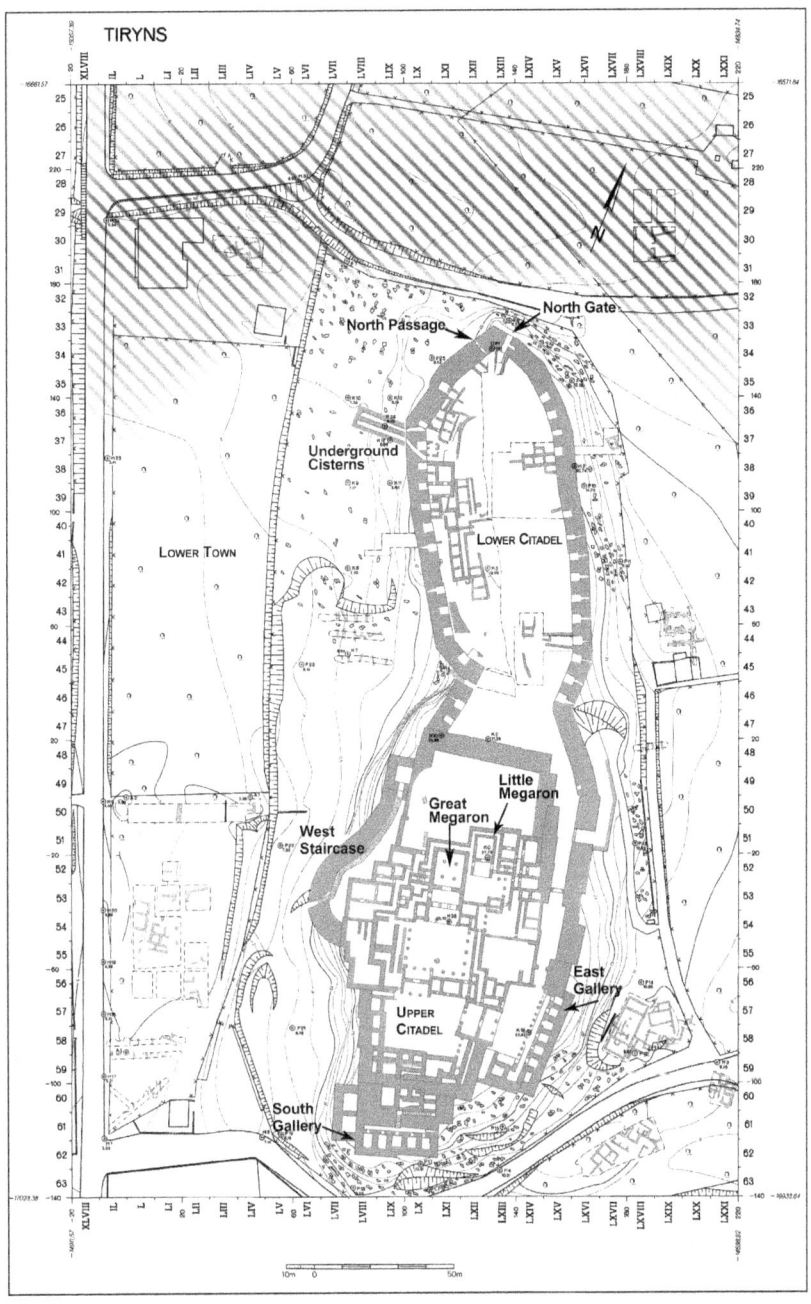

Figure 6 Plan of Late Palatial Tiryns (ca. 1250–1200 BCE) with estimated distribution of stream deposits (hatched) to the north of the Acropolis. Graphics: Tiryns-Project, M. Kostoula. Courtesy of Joseph Maran.

Livieratou & Thomatos 2009: 63–75; Mühlenbruch 2013; Maran 2016). In the Lower Citadel, the large and robust, two-storied houses of the LH IIIB period give way to single-storied one- and two-room houses, densely clustered around courtyards in a way recalling Mycenaean nonpalatial sites like Nichoria. A similar – albeit less densely built – layout is identifiable in the Lower Town of Tiryns (i.e., outside the citadel), which extends over 24.5 ha (i.e., is larger than in palatial times, and larger than Mycenaean Pylos), and may show evidence for urban planning (Maran 2016; Thaler 2020: 391).

Leaving Tiryns aside, in LH IIIC evidence of growth is typically only seen in regions which were not integrated into the palatial socio-economic system, such as Achaia (Giannopoulos 2007: 201–52; Moschos 2009), or which lay along its fringes, such as the Euboean Gulf (Lemos 2014: 169–74; Kramer-Hajos 2016: 149–65; Van Damme 2017; Knodell 2021: 138–41). Lefkandi is one of several Gulf sites (Kynos, Mitrou) which flourished in this period, probably thanks to maritime activity, from trade to raiding and piracy. Such activity is also assumed from two islets located further south, off the coast of Attica, in the same period (Murray & Lis 2023). Occupying a peninsula and commanding two harbors, the settlement of Lefkandi Xeropolis was a minor Mycenaean site under the orbit of the palace of Thebes (Lemos 2012: 22–23), but grew considerably in the Postpalatial period to reach 8–9 ha and become one of the largest LH IIIC settlements (Evely 2006; Lemos 2012: 22–3; 2014: 171–4). The buildings on Lefkandi Xeropolis, large houses divided by alleys and occasionally furnished with a second floor, show a specific orientation, which does not apply, however, to a large rectangular building ("Megaron") that dates from the twelfth and eleventh centuries and may have been the seat of a *basileus* (Lemos 2012: 23–4; 2014: 171–4; Kõiv 2016: 302–3; cf. Middleton 2010: 108–9).

Protogeometric settlement remains are represented much more thinly, and, for this period, we miss settlement plans altogether (Lemos 2002: 135–50; Jazwa 2019: 162). Scattered habitation is generally assumed, with examples ranging from Stamna in Aetolia (Christakopoulou-Somakou 2009: 1311–3) to Kavousi in Crete (Haggis 1993; 2013b: 66–71). However, there is considerable uncertainty, best exemplified by Athens. To most scholars, following the collapse, Athens was reduced to small habitation nuclei formed by clusters of houses linked to burial plots (e.g., Morris 1987: 62–5; Alexandridou 2020: 748; Rönnberg 2021: 111–4). However, Papadopoulos argues instead for a nucleated settlement concentrated on the Acropolis (Papadopoulos 2003: 297–316; Papadopoulos & Smithson 2017: 1, 10–12, 981–4).

"Most of the PG [Protogeometric] sites found are on top of, or close to, LBA sites," and LBA buildings are occasionally reused in Postpalatial times (Lemos 2002: 149). However, Protogeometric houses on the mainland are considerably smaller in size and different in construction techniques and spatial organization than their predecessors (Jazwa 2019). These free-standing, often single-room buildings, made of mudbrick or wattle-and-daub, are of apsidal (or oval) plan and were covered by pitched and probably thatched roofs (Fagerström 1988: 99–110; Mazarakis Ainian 1997: 111–3, 271–2; Lemos 2002: 149; Thaler 2020: 394). The best-known, but also by far the largest and most elaborate example of the type is the Lefkandi Toumba building (see Section 3). Scholars debate whether the apsidal building form, which is attested in the Middle Helladic period and survived in peripheral areas of the Mycenaean culture in the LBA, reemerged in the EIA because of influence from the north (Gounaris 2007: 94–5; Jazwa 2019: 163–4), poorer living standards and flimsier building materials of the period (Snodgrass 1971: 369–70), or a form better suited to the thinly spaced settlement layouts of the time (Lemos 2002: 149–50).

In Crete, the collapse is associated with a change in settlement patterns: Minoan coastal and lowland sites were abandoned, and new, mostly smaller sites were established at upland and defensible locations (Nowicki 2000; 2025; Wallace 2010: 49–72; Pollard 2023). Very few major lowland sites, including Knossos and Phaistos, survived (Wallace 2010: 68–71; Kotsonas 2021; Pollard 2023: 117–23). Although the date of the destruction of the palace of Knossos remains debated, the site shows considerable settlement contraction in the LBA (Hatzaki & Kotsonas 2020: 1034–6; Pollard 2023: 113–4; Pollard & Whitelaw 2025, Table 2). Indeed, Todd Whitelaw's surface survey over the Knossos valley established that, following the late Neopalatial period, when Knossos may have extended over 115–130 ha, it shrank gradually to reach 20 ha in the thirteenth and twelfth centuries (Whitelaw 2000; Pollard & Whitelaw 2025). Although the latter estimate seems low (and is perhaps conditioned by problems in data recovery and diagnosticity), it is comparable to the estimates for most Mycenaean palatial centers of the Greek mainland. The same survey challenged previous ideas on the form and size of EIA Knossos and established that it revived in the tenth and ninth centuries and became a nucleated urban site which exceeded 50 ha and involved no outlying villages (Figure 7). Burial evidence of the period demonstrates that Knossos was one of the most widely connected communities of the Mediterranean (Kotsonas 2019; 2021: 60–3). This new understanding of EIA Knossos makes it "extremely large for a Greek Iron Age city" (Cline 2024: 144), and – together with burial evidence (Section 3) – revolutionizes our understanding of socio-political complexity in the alleged Dark Age by showing the existence of large and hierarchical communities.

Dozens of defensible settlements were established in Crete in the LM IIIC period, including Karphi, Kavousi Vronda and Kastro, Vrokastro, and Khalasmenos. Once called refuge sites, these settlements have been reinterpreted

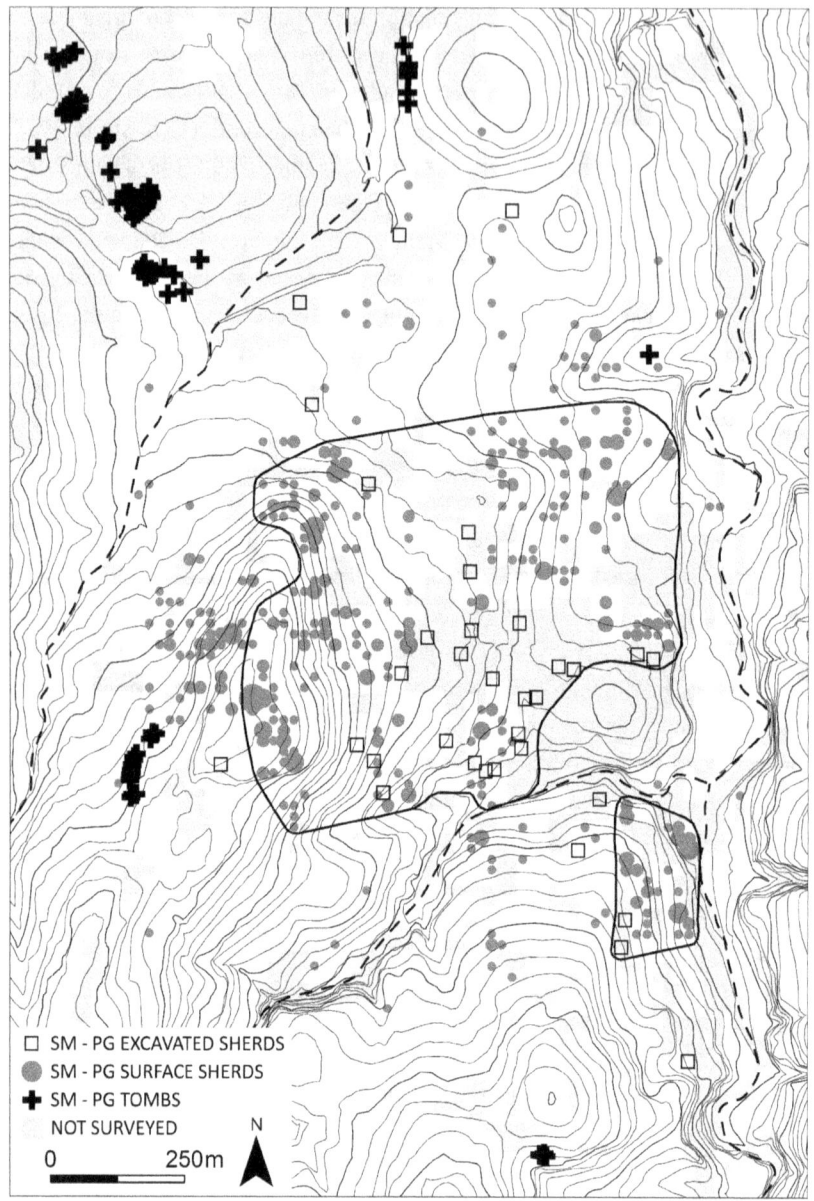

Figure 7 Knossos in the eleventh to ninth centuries, based on excavated data and the evidence from the Knossos Urban Landscape Project. Courtesy of Todd Whitelaw.

Social Change across the End of the Aegean Bronze Age 35

in ways which establish that the security considerations of their inhabitants were balanced with concerns over access to resources and site visibility (Nowicki 2000; 2025; Wallace 2010; Pollard 2023). Such sites are also attested in the Cyclades but remain rare elsewhere in Greece (Wallace 2010: 76–103). The Cretan defensible sites typically extend from 0.5 to 3 ha (Wallace 2010: 62, fig. 11) and show an often dense agglomeration of rectangular structures with flat roofs; these are multi-roomed houses that are arranged on natural or man-made terraces, separated by streets and courtyards, and probably developed progressively from an original core through agglutinative growth. Although mudbrick walls on stone foundations are common, as on the mainland, there are also stone walls (Wallace 2010: 105–8) (the more extensive use of stone and the flat roofs finds parallels on Cycladic sites). The overall layout and form of these settlements is a scaled-down version of that of Late Minoan towns, but there is less regularity and elaboration, and the buildings have fewer rooms (Dickinson 2006: 104–6; Wallace 2010: 113–4). Small LM IIIC sites can be located 0.5–1 km apart, the area of Kavousi in east Crete being a case in point. Based on historical analogy with pre-WWII occupation in that area, Donald Haggis (1993; 2013b: 66–71) argued that these sites are clusters of houses that represent kin groups closely linked socially and economically, and should thus be conceived as a single settlement unit; although each cluster could be abandoned periodically and reoccupied, the whole unit remained stable. Although Haggis (1993: 190–4) developed the Kavousi case study to explain the settlement record of EIA Greece, others have questioned the applicability of this model beyond east Crete (Whitley 2001: 88–9; Dickinson 2006: 90–3; Wallace 2010: 59–60; Pollard 2023: 122–3).

A possibly different settlement pattern can be inferred from the tiny site (0.04 ha) of Malia Pezoula in central Crete. Occupying a low rocky hill southwest of the Minoan town of Malia, it dates from the eleventh and tenth centuries and involves a compound of 16 rooms, standing in isolation (Mandalaki 2006; Kotsonas 2021: 59–60). Cretan settlements of comparable size are typically classified as farmsteads (Wallace 2010: 71–2, 332–6). If it is a farmstead (indeed, the first farmstead of the period to be fully excavated), Malia Pezoula could have been economically and politically dependent on a larger site (cf. Wallace 2010: 71–2), suggesting a level of settlement hierarchy that was previously undocumented (Kotsonas 2021: 59–60). In any case, Malia Pezoula and more than half of the Cretan settlements established in the twelfth century were abandoned by the tenth, when settlement expansion and nucleation occurred in a minority of sites, many of which eventually became the island's Classical poleis, such as Gortyn or Lyktos (Wallace 2010: 231–66; Pollard 2023: 123–8; Nowicki 2025, 221–2, 232–3).

The settlement record of EIA Greece has served the development of influential models of social structure. Based on a thorough survey of this record and an analysis of the Homeric epics, Alexander Mazarakis Ainian (1997) identified prominent houses as rulers' dwellings, thus challenging the impression that social hierarchy was lacking in this period. Both his focus on individual buildings and the all-embracing scope of his approach are susceptible to criticism. Indeed, Haggis (1993; 2013b) has argued that the subject of settlement and social structure in EIA Greece is best approached not at the level of the individual building or even the individual site, but at the level of the micro-region (on which see Horden & Purcell 2000). As he argues, this level is better suited to address localized shifts in settlement foci over time. Additionally, Whitley (1991b; and, more cautiously, in 2001: 89–90) has observed that, by relying on Homer and the impression of a uniform Homeric society, archaeologists fail to appreciate the diversity of settlement form and social structure in EIA Greece. To capture this diversity, Whitley introduced the distinction between long-lived/stable settlements, which were typically large and outlived the EIA, and short-lived/unstable settlements, often of small size. Whitley approached both settlement types in the light of ethnographic comparison and found that unstable settlements conformed to the "big man" model; they rose as charismatic leaders attracted followers, and were abandoned when their authority ended. An essential problem of this model lies in the polarities it is based on, which hark back to processual archaeology and French structuralism. Others have questioned the suitability of Whitley's ethnographic comparisons (e.g., Wallace 2010: 165), and have observed that the various unstable settlements he discusses (e.g., Kavousi Vronda, or Nichoria) lasted for considerably more than a generation or two, and were often abandoned over time, rather than abruptly (e.g., Dickinson 2006: 110–1; Wallace 2010: 165). Additionally, analysis of two Cretan short-lived settlements, Karphi and Kavousi Vronda, deduced different social structures (Day & Snyder 2004), thus hinting at notable diversity in settlement and social structure.

Although Whitley's model is no longer popular, his distinction between stable and unstable settlements of the Greek EIA informs the model of static and dynamic settlement structure developed by Haggis (2013a) for the Aegean Bronze Age and EIA. In his model, Haggis distinguishes between two different forms of settlement: one involving agglomerative constructions characterized by constancy and additive expansion, and another encompassing freestanding buildings showing discontinuous expansion through episodes of destruction. Haggis associates each of these forms with different models of socio-political organization: group-oriented, heterarchical, with staple finance, on the one hand, and individual-oriented, hierarchical, with wealth finance, on the other.

Although these polarities recall those developed by Whitley, Haggis's model is more flexible: in theory, a site can show a static structure in one period, and a dynamic one in another, with obvious implications for social change. Additionally, Haggis's model is innovative in associating the phenomenology of social structures with their imprint on site formation processes. The same model relates to funerary evidence (Haggis relates his former structure with extramural and collective burial, and the latter intramural and individual burial), to which I now turn.

7 Burials and Social Change

Burials have been the most extensively explored and published data from preClassical Greece. However, most graves (perhaps 90%) are investigated hastily in salvage operations (Galanakis 2020: 350), and final publications remain scarce, with only 5% of the LBA and EIA burials excavated since WW II possibly published to date (Galanakis 2020: 369). Leaving aside the case of Athens and the Argolid, which have received extensive attention (Pappi 2014; Papadopoulos & Smithson 2017; Dimitriadou 2019; Rönnberg 2021: 167–216), final publications of large burial assemblages of IIIC to Protogeometric date are largely limited to Knossos (Brock 1957; Coldstream & Catling 1996), Perati (Iakovidis 1969–70), Lefkandi (Popham, Sackett, & Themelis 1980; Popham, Calligas, & Sackett 1993), Torone (Papadopoulos 2005), Stamna (Christakopoulou-Somakou 2009), and Kavousi Vronda (Preston Day & Liston 2023). This is only a fraction of the burial sites of the period known from across the central Aegean (Lemos 2002: 152–84; Thomatos 2006: 149–66), Crete (Eaby 2007), Thessaly (Karouzou 2018, 137–73), and Macedonia (Chemssedoha 2019).

Scholarship has long focused on the description, dating, and classification of Greek burial remains, and the interpretation of funerary customs in the light of texts and iconography (Kurtz & Boardman 1971; Vermeule 1979; Kountouri & Gadolou 2019). Any social inferences were largely limited to the identification of the graves of "heroes" (Hattler 2008) and "princesses" (Stampolidis 2012). Scholars have rightly identified the gender biases in this approach (Harrell 2014) and have developed more nuanced social and demographic inquiries. Snodgrass (1977) used quantitative analysis of burial to trace the rise of the polis, while Ian Morris (1987) and James Whitley (1991a) revisited the topic through processual archaeological approaches. Notwithstanding criticism of their methods and historical interpretations (e.g. Papadopoulos 1993; Dickinson 2006: 174–8; Rönnberg 2021: 201–6), the works of Whitley, and especially Morris, were exceptionally successful in raising fresh questions over burial and social structure, including demography, access to formal burial, and the significance of grave goods. In the last two decades, Aegean burials have attracted a range of contextual and postprocessual considerations centered on the performance and negotiation of personhood and embodied identities (Dakouri-Hild & Boyd 2016; Mina, Triantaphyllou & Papadatos 2016), which relate to broader conversations over burial and social change (Norstein & Selsvold 2025).

These recent theoretical advances are matched by advances in the excavation and study of human remains. Physical anthropological studies on EIA graves (in the Athenian Agora and the Kerameikos) first appeared in 1939, and were introduced elsewhere in the Aegean from the 1980s (Papadopoulou 2017: 606–15). In the last decades, burial archaeology in Greece encompasses bioarchaeological and environmental analyses (e.g., Tarlow & Nilsson Stutz 2013: Part II) to archaeothanatology (Duday 2009), and sheds new light on palaeopathology and subsistence (Morris 2007: 222–4; Lemos 2022: 22, with references). Although such research is rarely applied in most excavations of Greek cemeteries (e.g., Kountouri & Gadolou 2019), the few case studies available to date offer invaluable insights into social change.

The burial record of the Mycenaean Palatial period is fairly consistent in terms of tomb placement, architecture, and burial assemblages, notwithstanding regional and site-specific variation (Cavanagh & Mee 1998: 61–88; Dickinson 2006: 38–9; Galanakis 2020: 363). Inhumation is almost universal. Burials are typically grouped in cemeteries, including different tomb types, one of which, typically the rock-cut chamber tomb, is usually dominant. In the Mycenaean Palatial period, monumental tholos tombs are fewer than in earlier times and are built around major sites (Galanakis 2020: 356–7, 362), while cists, pits, and other simple forms are also attested (Lewartowski 2000). Chamber and tholos tombs were used for multiple burials, which were placed on the grave floor or in a pit or niche constructed within the grave. Grave goods present considerable variation not only between sites and tomb types, but also across the same site and across specimens of the same tomb type, and between burials within a collective tomb. Tholoi represent the highest level of investment and are typically ascribed to a narrow elite, while chamber tombs can belong to either elite or nonelite groups (Cavanagh & Mee 1998: 78; Galanakis 2020: 351). Burials in cists and pits, which are rarer in the Mycenaean Palatial period than in earlier or later times, and have proportionally higher chances for holding no burial offerings, were often attributed to a lower social stratum than chamber-tomb users. However, this attribution is questionable, and such sparsely represented tomb types are unlikely to represent any specific social class (Lewartowski 2000: 13–4, 18, 47–51).

Skeletal and stable isotope analysis on Mycenaean burials from Pylos and elsewhere demonstrate that people of different status – as inferred from tomb type – and gender had different diets (Schepartz et al. 2017). Indeed, individuals buried in Pylian tholoi had the highest levels of animal protein, while men systematically had better dental health than women across different tomb types. Likewise, the women of East Lokris suffered more from nutritional issues and metabolic disorders than the men, both before and after the collapse (Iezzi 2009). Nevertheless, stable carbon and nitrogen isotope analysis conducted on two Protogeometric cemeteries at Pharsala, Thessaly, established that animal protein occupied a significant part of the diet of the people, and did not depend on status and gender (Panagiotopoulou et al. 2018b).

Funerary iconography from both the Palatial and Postpalatial periods portrays women as mourners (Olsen 2020: 298–300). However, Greek EIA female burials present no recurrent attestation of specific artifacts (with the exception of Athens; see Whitley 1996: 214, 219; contra Papadopoulos & Smithson 2017: 664), which has been taken to suggest that gendered divisions of the time are not so much between adult men and women as between male warriors on the one hand and sexually undifferentiated children on the other (Whitley 1996: 220).

Patterns of continuity and change from the LBA to the EIA are also identifiable in the use of tomb types. The range of Mycenaean types largely persists, but they show remarkable changes in use (Cavanagh & Mee 1998: 89–97, 135; Dickinson 2006: 73; Thomatos 2006: 149–78; Bulmer 2020; Galanakis 2020: 363–4). Many tholos and chamber tombs are abandoned, and the construction of new such tombs peters out. Also, newly cut chamber tombs are typically smaller in size, hold fewer burials, and extend over shorter periods, as exemplified by Perati (Figure 8; Iakovidis 1969–70). All this has been taken to suggest "a society in dissolution" (Cavanagh & Mee 1998: 135).

The establishment of new cemeteries in the twelfth and eleventh centuries has often been attributed to the arrival of new populations, but it is more likely to reflect social change, as hypothesized for the Knossos North Cemetery (see Section 3). The influx of small groups of people from Cyprus and of talismanic beliefs from the Eastern Mediterranean, which have been identified in the burial record of Perati and Lefkandi respectively (Arrington 2016; Murray 2018b), is indicative of the transformative impact of overseas connections on coastal communities. Nevertheless, an analytical approach to Thessalian cemeteries established the local origins of nearly all the population, thus calling into question any assumption of extensive mobility (Panagiotopoulou et al. 2018a).

The pronounced regional and site-specific variation of burial in the IIIC and Protogeometric periods (Lemos 2002: 151–90; Thomatos 2006: 149–78) cannot possibly be captured in this brief section, which focuses instead on two

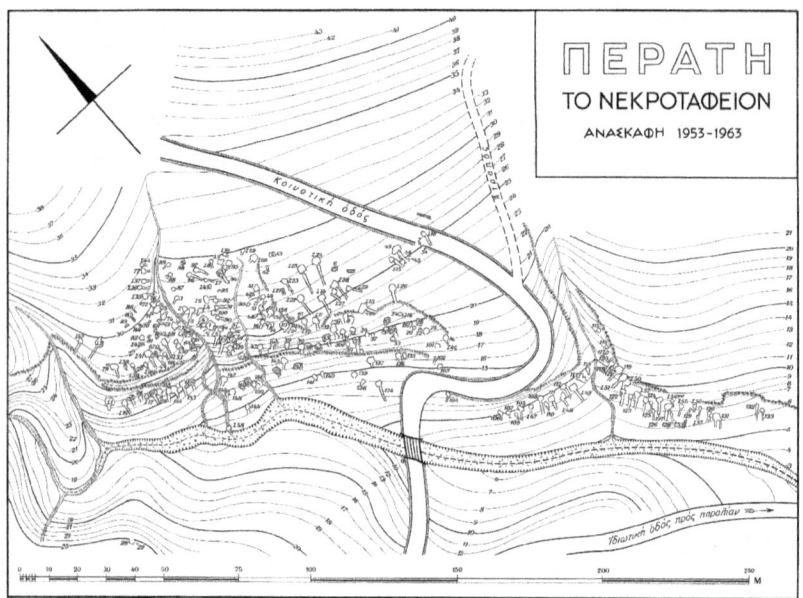

Figure 8 Plan of the Postpalatial cemetery of Perati (from Iakovidis 1969, plan 1). © Archive of the Archaeological Society at Athens.

novelties of the periods – the shift from collective to single burial and the introduction of cremation (for the additional novelty of warrior graves, see Section 3) – and the debates over their significance as markers of ethnic/racial or social change.

The shift to single burial began gradually in the LH IIIC period, before culminating in the Submycenaean (Lewartowski 2000: 11–2, table 3; Lemos 2002: 185; Dickinson 2006: 181–3; Thomatos 2006: 170; Bulmer 2020: 149). "By the beginning of the PG period, the universal practice is single burials," but chamber tombs and small tholoi are attested in Crete, Messenia, Thessaly, and some Central Greek sites (Lemos 2002: 186). Collective burial in tumuli persisted in Epirus and Macedonia (Andreou & Kleitsas 2018; Chemsseddoha 2019: 74–88). Desborough took the shift to single burial as a symptom for "the rejection of the Mycenaean way of life" and ascribed it to "the arrival of newcomers who fused with, and dominated, the surviving element" (Desborough 1972: 109; cf. 1964: 37–40; like–minded literature is referenced in Hall 1997: 117; Papadopoulos & Smithson 2017: 685). Snodgrass (1971: 184–6) and others (cited in Lemos 2002: 185, fn. 383) were critical of this idea, and of the craniometric evidence occasionally used to support it. He argued instead that the spread of single burial represented the revival of a Middle Helladic practice, which had grown unpopular in Palatial times but survived in peripheral areas; he ascribed this revival to a substratum of the population, which reemerged after the palatial elites had disappeared (Snodgrass 1971: 186–7; 2002; cf. Desborough 1972: 108: 269–70; Hooker 1976: 179). The idea has attracted skepticism (Morris 2000: 200–1), and Lemos (2002: 185–6) has proposed that the shift to single burial was caused by the arrival of both people and ideas from the northern periphery of the Mycenaean world. Notwithstanding the different arguments, scholarship agrees that the shift to single burial came as a response to the instability and mobility of the population of the Postpalatial period, which discouraged investment in larger, potentially multi-generational tombs (Snodgrass 1971: 186–7; Desborough 1972: 108; cf. Lemos 2002: 185; Thomatos 2006: 169). Social considerations also pertain to Haggis's (2013a) treatment of single and collective burial as correlates of the phenomenology of dynamic and static social structure. Economics may have played a role as well, as evidenced, for example, by the decreased size of the tholoi and chamber tombs built in this period (Dickinson 2006: 189). In any case, the shift to single burial must have involved a change in ritual, especially since it involved the abandonment of the Mycenaean custom of reopening collective tombs and repositioning the bones of earlier burials (Thomatos 2006: 169–70).

Changes in ritual also pertain to the introduction of cremation, the significance of which has long divided scholars. Cremation is very rarely attested in prehistoric Greece both over time and space; it is only in the LM IIIC period that the rite began to be practiced regularly, especially by coastal communities around the Aegean, including the northern Peloponnese, Attica, Thebes, Rhodes, Kos, and east and central Crete (Iakovidis 1969–70:B: 43–56; Stampolidis 2001; Thomatos 2006: 170–4, maps 5–7; Ruppenstein 2013: 186, figure 1). In the Protogeometric period, cremation became the dominant rite in Athens and perhaps at Lefkandi (Lemos 2002: 186), but remained extremely rare on the Aegean islands, except for Crete, Rhodes, and Naxos (Kaklamani 2021: 14–6, map 1, table 1).

The introduction of cremation was once credited to the Dorians or to unspecified northern invaders (Hall 1997: 116–7, with references). This idea has been dismissed since the 1970s (Kurtz & Boardman 1971: 33; Desborough 1972: 275), since the contexts of IIIC cremations present no intrusive features (Thomatos 2006: 177), while their distribution does not conform to the geography of the alleged Dorian migration and to any geographic patterning relatable to migration. Accordingly, most scholars maintain that cremation spread through interregional contact (e.g., Cavanagh & Mee 1998: 97; Dickinson 2006: 180; Bulmer 2020: 147). This could have involved the mobility of individuals, as indicated by recent strontium analyses of a few LH IIIC cremations in the

Argolid (mentioned by Niki Papakonstantinou and Dimitra-Ermioni Michael in Triantafyllou 2025). This is one of the major findings on Aegean cremation, which is emerging from the bio-anthropological *TEFRA* project of Sevi Triantafyllou (Aristotle University of Thessaloniki) that investigates the technology and social context of the use of fire on human remains.

Older literature traces the source of inspiration for Aegean cremations of the period to Anatolia or – less likely – the Levantine coast (e.g. Iakovidis 1969–70: B: 56–7; Snodgrass 1971: 189, 326–7; Lemos 2002: 186; Thomatos 2006: 174–6, maps 8–11; *contra* Ruppenstein 2013: 188; Papadopoulos & Smithson 2017: 679); however, individual studies of the last two decades hypothesize Balkan, Italian, and even Iberian origins (Ruppenstein 2013: 187–90; Kaklamani 2021: 1–2, with references). In any case, a single source of inspiration could hardly account for the various types of cremation manifested in the period (Ruppenstein 2013; Papadopoulos & Smithson 2017: 679–80), and this variety also hints at diverse motivations for the adoption of the rite.

Postpalatial cremations are often found in chamber tombs together with inhumations, which suggests that "there were neither family nor religious objections to the practice" (Desborough 1972: 268; cf. Snodgrass 1971: 146; Lemos 2002: 186; Dickinson 2006: 180). Some hypothesize that the spread of cremation was inspired from stories for heroes such as those in the Homeric epic, and/or associate it with the "warrior graves" which characterize the period (Kaklamani 2021: 2, with references; also, Section 3), like the burials at Knossos and Lefkandi discussed above; yet, a good portion of the early cremations show no weapons or heroic paraphernalia. Additionally, the osteoarcheological analyses of cremated bones from LH IIIC Perati and Subminoan–Protogeometric Lefkandi demonstrate that the rite was used for both sexes and different age groups (Lemos 2002: 186). Thus, since the 1970s, the introduction of cremation is widely considered as a matter of social fashion (Kurtz & Boardman 1971: 37; Snodgrass 1971: 146–7; Desborough 1972: 275; Papadopoulos & Smithson 2017: 679–80). Some observe that cremations of the period often yield no richer offerings than inhumations (Dickinson 2006: 181, 189; Kaklamani 2021: 2), but degrees of investment cannot be evaluated solely based on the inorganic materials preserved in a grave. Indeed, the approximately one ton of fuel and the associated labor required for cremation suggest that this rite may have been an elite prerogative (Lemos 2002: 186–7; Dickinson 2006: 181; Thomatos 2006: 177; Bulmer 2020: 146). Anyway, the performance of cremation was a longer and probably stronger sensorial experience for the kin and kith of the deceased (Lemos 2002: 187; Kaklamani 2021: 193–4). Additionally, the ostentatious destruction of bodies and objects which this rite involved may be indicative of new ideas about personhood and human-thing entanglements, which can also be identified in the Homeric epics (Whitley 2002; 2012; 2016). Interestingly, new ideas about personhood have also been deduced from LH IIIC collective tombs with inhumations (Moutafi 2021: 275, 282). Taken together, this evidence sketches a little-known but potentially crucial aspect of social change in the aftermath of the collapse.

8 Sanctuaries and Social Change

In the Hollywood comedy *Bruce Almighty* (2003), God leaves his powers to a common man and goes on vacation. When the baffled man asks how it is possible for God to do so, He replies, "Did you ever hear of the Dark Ages?" The notion that gods or rather sanctuaries disappeared from the Aegean during the Greek "Dark Age(s)" became firmly established in scholarship in the 1970s (Snodgrass 1971: 394–401, 408–13, 421–3; Desborough 1972: 278–87; Burkert 1977: 88–98; Coldstream 1977: 317–39). This consensus revised the influential conclusions which Martin Nilsson had drawn half a century earlier, which held "that there is very strong cumulative evidence for the continuity of Mycenaean cults in the Greek age" (Nilsson 1927: 414), and that the number and location of sanctuaries remained stable from the Bronze Age into the EIA (Nilsson 1927: 391–414). After another half century, the consensus of the 1970s over the "twilight of the gods" and the demise of sanctuaries deserves to be revisited in the light of enduring discussions over continuity and change in Greek religion across the end of the Bronze Age (Prent 2005; Lupack 2020; with criticism in Whitley 2009).

Because of their nature as administrative documents, the Mycenaean Linear B tablets do not offer many insights into religion, beyond recording the who, where, and how of the offerings made to numerous divinities mentioned by name (Bendall 2007; Rutherford 2013: 258). When texts reappear, from the works of Homer and Hesiod onward, some of the divine names attested in Linear B are identifiable as Olympian gods (Zeus, Hera, Poseidon, Hermes, Ares?, Dionysos, Artemis, Athena), as lesser divine figures (e.g., Erinys), or as divine epithets (e.g., Enyalios, Paion, Potnia); however, a host of other names of Mycenaean divinities are not attested in Classical religion, which indicates their disappearance in the centuries that followed the collapse and suggests profound religious change (Dickinson 2006: 223–4; Rutherford 2013: 260–1, 271; Lupack 2020: 164–5; Cosmopoulos 2025: 217–33). Given the brief references of the tablets, the Mycenaean divine names cannot be securely identified with images of divinities attested in the visual arts of the LBA (Rutherford 2013: 261–2). This is unlike the figures rendered in the Greek visual arts of the eighth and especially the seventh centuries, which can often be securely associated with divinities known from contemporary and later literature (Burkert 1977: 191–9). For the intervening period of the twelfth to ninth centuries, we have no textual record and thus no names of divinities. However, the thin scatter of images of divinities available for this period is largely on objects imported from the Near East and Egypt, and renders nonGreek gods (Jantzen 1972; Renfrew 1985: 303–10; Hölbl 2015). The cultural significance of this phenomenon and its potential impact on Greek religion has barely been appreciated to date (but see Paizi forthcoming), even by the few scholars who argue for notable Near Eastern impact on Greek religion earlier in the 2nd millennium (e.g., Kirk 1990: 2–8; *contra* Dickinson 2006: 221–2).

Probably more straightforward is the question of the demise of sanctuaries after the palatial collapse. Desborough (1964: 40–7) struggled to identify any continuity of cult across the end of the Bronze Age. The seminal publications of the 1970s mapped and quantified the relevant data, thus establishing a strong impression of a very low number of sanctuaries between ca. 1200 BCE and the eighth century Renaissance, when a sixfold increase in their number was identified by Coldstream (1977: 317–20). However, both the premises and primary data which underlie this approach call for reconsideration.

The empirical approach toward the identification of sanctuaries was challenged in the mid-1980s, when Renfrew (1985: 11–26) theorized the behavioral correlates of cultic activity. His approach has been influential, especially with scholars studying periods of low archaeological visibility, including the earliest part of the EIA (Morgan 1999: 295–343; Marakas 2010: 7–14). To explain the low visibility of cult in this period, François De Polignac (1984: 27–31) argued for its spatial indeterminacy. Drawing attention to the Homeric description (*Odyssey* 3.5–6) of a sacrifice on a beach which presents no altar or other structure, De Polignac argued that in this period cult was focused on sacred practice, rather than sacred space. Another model developed by Mazarakis Ainian (1997: esp. 340–96) sought to explain the low visibility of cult in this period by postulating that ritual was conducted in rulers' dwellings, which means that its material record is intermingled with domestic remains, and is therefore hard to discern. These two influential models have attracted wide-ranging criticism (Sourvinou-Inwood 1993; Whitley 2001: 138–9; Dickinson 2006: 236; Pierattini 2022a: 4–7, 41–6), which, however, has not targeted the quantitative data on which they are based. My updated review of this data has exposed considerable departures from previous estimates: the number of EIA sanctuaries is much higher than previously thought and remains relatively stable from 1050 to 750 BCE, while the increase from the mid-eighth century remains pronounced, but it is roughly half as strong as Coldstream suggested (Kotsonas 2017: 58–9, fig. 1). Additionally, I have shown that the revised number and geographical distribution of sanctuaries in eleventh and tenth century Greece (Kotsonas 2017: 58–60, figs. 1–2) does not confirm the impression of any serious demise and largely conforms to patterns seen in the LBA Aegean (on which see Whittaker 1997: 8–65, tables 1 and 15): Crete boast numerous sanctuaries, the Peloponnese comes second, the Cyclades follow, and a few other regions are represented thinly. Set against the background of the LBA, the overall number and regional distribution of Greek EIA sanctuaries seems unaffected by the collapse (Kotsonas 2017: 62; Pierattini 2022a: 21). Although numerous cult sites were abandoned ca. 1200 BCE, others emerged elsewhere in the same region.

To fully appreciate these ramifications, one needs to look beyond quantitative data. Below, I discuss qualitative aspects of the form and function of sanctuaries before and after the collapse.

According to Jim Wright, cult places of the Palatial period conform to three types: a) the megaron of the palaces, where rituals were conducted and were probably officiated by the *wanax*; b) specialized cult centers located within citadels and attached to palaces (e.g., at Mycenae); and c) sanctuaries at nonpalatial sites (e.g., Amyklaion, Epidauros/Maleatas) (Wright 1994: 54–72; cf. Rutherford 2013: 259, 263–4). Gemma Marakas (2010: 72–80) introduced a somewhat different, yet still tripartite typology for the sanctuaries of the Mycenaean Palatial to Protogeometric periods: a) palatial shrines (like the Cult Center of Mycenae), b) shrines at nonpalatial settlements (e.g., Agia Irene, Epidauros/Maleatas, Phylakopi), and c) isolated shrines (e.g., Amyklaion, Kalapodi). More recently, Birgitta Eder (2019) developed a five-fold classification for the sanctuaries of the same period. To Wright's types a and b, Eder added settlement sanctuaries (=Marakas type b), and "extra-urban" shrines located either on crossroads/mountain passes (e.g., Ayios Konstantinos at Methana), or on peaks (e.g., Mounts Arachnaion and Lykaion). Based on discoveries of the last decades, Eder drew a contrast between extra-urban sanctuaries, which lack elite offerings but retained prominence throughout this period, and sanctuaries situated within palaces and near them, which were favored by the palatial court but disappeared with the collapse or within the Postpalatial period (cf. Lupack 2020: 162, 165–6). She further observed that settlement sanctuaries are thinly represented on the mainland throughout the period in question, with the exception of Postpalatial Tiryns (Mühlenbruch 2013) and perhaps the "Ritual Zone" at Lefkandi Xeropolis (Lemos & Tsingarida 2019). Notwithstanding their merits, these typological studies retain an exclusive focus on the southern Greek mainland, with only Marakas also covering the Cyclades (cf. Rousioti 2018). The exclusion of Crete and the Cretan types of cult sites (which include peculiarities such as cave sanctuaries) – typically explained by the profound impact of Minoan religion on the island's later cultic landscape (Snodgrass 1971: 394–401; Desborough 1972: 278–87; Coldstream 1977: 327–32; Lemos 2002: 222–4; Dickinson 2006: 224–6; Whitley 2009) – not only fuels the problematic notion of Cretan religious exceptionalism (Haysom 2011), but also has a limiting effect on the comprehensive study of Aegean cult practice across the end of the Bronze Age. The following paragraphs can only touch upon major aspects of this topic by elaborating on the above typologies.

The megaron of the Mycenaean palaces was the focus of the hearth-*wanax* ideology, which treated the hearth as the center of the state and the *wanax* as its father and chief (Wright 1994: 57–9; cf. Marakas 2010: 98–102). The architecture and wall-paintings of the palaces invested the rituals practiced there in supernatural power and mythologized social realities (Wright 1994: 57–60; Haysom 2020: 322). Beyond the megaron, Mycenaean sacred architecture is characterized by a lack of canonization and monumentality (Whittaker 1997: esp. 26; Thaler 2020: 382). This is evidenced by its best-known example, that is, the Cult Center of Mycenae, which encompasses five cult buildings that are arranged around a courtyard, are of modest size and irregular plan, and show only a few elements of palatial architecture, such as monolithic thresholds, columns, or wall paintings (Haysom 2020: 319; Thaler 2020: 382). The contents of the rooms include benches, platforms, and other features, and terracotta figures and figurines. Given its small size and location within the citadel, the complex could have accommodated only exclusive groups of a few dozen people (Haysom 2020: 321). Small shrines featuring main rooms and rear rooms, benches, terracotta figures, and other ritual objects are attested elsewhere on the Greek mainland, the Cyclades, and Crete (Whittaker 1997: 8–65; Rousioti 2018; Haysom 2020: 324; 2024), with examples including Ayios Konstantinos at Methana (Hamilakis & Konsolaki 2004) and Phylakopi on Melos (e.g., Renfrew 1985). Other Mycenaean sanctuaries are extra-urban and open-air, and show concentrations of figurines (Haysom 2020: 323–4). Kalapodi is exceptional in being an extra-urban Mycenaean sanctuary with two successive temples enclosing an altar and a platform (Niemeier 2016: 7–10; Pierattini 2022a: 31–35).

The Linear B tablets record that the *wanax*, magistrates, and communities sent various offerings – including oil, wine, honey, cereals, animals and animal products – to sanctuaries, which recalls wall paintings from Thebes and Pylos illustrating processions of people holdings offerings (Bendall 2007; Rutherford 2013: 264, 268; Lupack 2011; 2020: 163–4; Pratt 2021: 124–8). While the resources devoted to religion were only a small proportion of those over which the palace had oversight (and an even smaller proportion of the overall economy), disbursements for religious purposes form a very large proportion of all the final disbursements recorded in the tablets, which suggests the investment of palatial administration in religion. Contrary to what earlier scholars held, burnt animal sacrifice is attested in this Palatial period (Hamilakis & Konsolaki 2004; cf. Dickinson 2006: 223–4; Rutherford 2013: 266; Lupack 2020: 163), even if much more rarely than in Postpalatial and later times (Cosmopoulos 2025: 237–9).

Following the collapse, the megaron and its religious trappings disappeared. Although Building T, which was built over the megaron at Tiryns, retained its form, it lacked any hearth and wall-paintings, which is indicative of the disappearance of the hearth-*wanax* ideology and of profound social change (Maran 2000; 2012). An altar facing Building T, and open-air hearths at Tiryns and Mycenae are indicative of the persistence of ritual in former palatial sites, with the possible participation of much larger audiences (Haysom 2020: 326–7). Bench sanctuaries and open-air sanctuaries continue and expand considerably during this period (Haysom 2020: 325; 2024; Thaler 2020: 382–3, 388). While bench sanctuaries disappear thereafter from the mainland, Cretan bench sanctuaries continue into the Protogeometric period. The Cretan examples typically show a standardized set of clay objects (Figure 9), including "goddesses with upraised arms" (which may actually represent female votaries), tubular stands, kalathoi holding foodstuffs, and plaques (Prent 2005: 126–54, 174–8, 181–4, 188–200; Gaignerot-Driessen 2014). At Karphi, this set is found in a temple, but components of it are also represented across the site, which encourages the shifting of scholarly focus from the assumed ritual character of the objects and the spaces in which they are found to the range of practices these objects could have been involved in (Haysom 2019).

Figure 9 Ritual objects from Cretan bench sanctuaries, especially of the Postpalatial period. Archaeological Museum of Heraklion. © Hellenic Ministry of Culture – Hellenic Organisation of Cultural Resources.

Cretan open-air and cave sanctuaries, which typically have a long history (Prent 2005: 154–74, 178, 184–7, 200–9), yield no sets of such objects but individual specimens, in addition to clay and bronze figurines (the latter being well attested in Minoan Crete, but being very rare on the mainland before the turn of the millennium; see Lebessi 2002; Murray 2022), and items of personal adornment. Exceptional are the clay figurines of kourotrophoi, heterosexual couples, and pregnant women from the cave sanctuary of the childbirth goddess Eileithyia at Inatos (Kanta, Davaras, & Betancourt 2022), especially since the latter two schemes are unparalleled in Aegean LBA art (Olsen 2020: 301). These Cretan sanctuaries may have lost their broader regional role during the LBA/EIA transition, but in the well-studied case of Syme Viannou, this role resumed from the Protogeometric period, when the cult of Hermes and Aphrodite was introduced and maturation rituals for young males were established (Lebessi 2002: 4–5, 270–82; Kotsonas 2024: 548–52). The terracottas from Syme Viannou and Inatos suggest a new emphasis on gender roles and human reproduction in Cretan sanctuaries. Social change of this sort is also inferred from a tenth-century krater from Sybrita that shows armed men dancing (D'Agata 2012).

Open-air sanctuaries are less commonly attested on the mainland, though they have proven less exceptional than once thought (Pierattini 2022a: 22–3). Some of them present an interruption of cult practice ca. 1200 BCE (e.g. Eleusis and Epidauros/Maleatas; see Cosmopoulos 2014; Pierattini 2022a: 22–3), others show continuity of cult (e.g. Kalapodi; see Niemeier 2016; Pierattini 2022a: 31–5), and yet others, such as Olympia (Kyrieleis 2006), Isthmia (Morgan 1999), and the Amyklaion (Vlachou 2024: 321–2, 326–9), were first established in the twelfth–eleventh centuries, in prominent positions for their thinly connected regional settlement networks, to serve as venues for the gathering and social interaction of local communities and their leaders (Morgan 1999: esp. 369–86; Haysom 2020: 329–32). The open-air sanctuaries of the period are characterized by ash deposits, animal bones and pottery which are indicative of sacrifices and ritualized dining (Morgan 1999: esp. 369–86; also, Lemos 2002: 221–4; Kyrieleis 2006; Pratt 2021: 210–2). Figurines and metal objects (including items of personal adornment at first, and later tripod cauldrons at select sites) are attested rarely in this period but increase markedly in later centuries (Morgan 1999: 389–94; Dickinson 2006: 235–6).

Greek cult buildings and altars remain rare and architecturally unassuming before the eighth century, but they are attested in different Greek regions (Kotsonas 2017: 60–2, fig. 3–4; Pierattini 2022a: 21–55; Morgan 2024). The discovery of a sequence of Mycenaean to Roman temples at Kalapodi revolutionized our understanding of early Greek sanctuary architecture. The form of the earliest of these structures is not well preserved, but phase 4 of the South Temple includes an early tenth-century apsidal structure surrounded by a wooden colonnade, which recalls the building at Lefkandi Toumba (Niemeier 2016: 12–3; Pierattini 2022a: 324). The argument that the Greek cult buildings of LBA and/or the EIA, followed – architecturally and conceptually (as abodes of the gods) – Syro-Palestinian models is considered unconvincing (Whittaker 1997: 66–93; Pierattini 2022a: 46–9). In any case, the performance of ritual by presumably exclusive elite groups within architecturally confined spaces, which characterized Mycenaean palatial religion, disappeared with the collapse. Thereafter, open-air sanctuaries, which were traditionally accessible to wider segments of the population, gained prominence. This development is symptomatic of broader patterns of social change manifested in this period.

9 Conclusions

For a long time, the LBA/EIA transition was overshadowed by an emphasis on other periods of Aegean archaeology, and/or fell under the purview of "revolution and catastrophe history" (Horden & Purcell 2000: 367). However, the intensification of research over the last half century has generated a wealth of new data and increasingly nuanced approaches.

When the wealth of new data is quantified (e.g., in Sections 4 and 8, on demography and sanctuaries), it establishes that past quantifications have grossly exaggerated the evidence for decline and rupture. This finding not only undercuts traditional understandings of the period as a Dark Age, and the range of linear and polarizing interpretative models which apply to it (Sections 3–7); it also invites us to contextualize longstanding discussions over continuity and change across these periods (as promoted in Whitley 2009), and transform the understanding of the nature, context, and degree of social change. In arguing accordingly, I do not deny that the collapse took a toll on much of Greece, but I call for this impression to be qualified and contextualized. Indeed, there is reason to think that the aftermath of the collapse may have been much shorter than previously considered (e.g. Dickinson 2006: 238–58), as explained in the discussion of absolute chronology in the Appendix. Additionally, it is increasingly acknowledged that the collapse had an uneven impact on different regions, communities, and social groups, this impact being often conditioned by the degree to which these entities were integrated into the Mycenaean palatial orbit. To capture and interpret this variability, we depend on the expansion of our primary datasets, which is hampered by the problem of unpublished excavations (cf. Knodell 2021: 244–5), especially of nonburial sites. This problem is shaped not only by the logistical challenges of the herculean task of conducting fieldwork and bringing it to final publication, but also by the unsatisfactory institutional support – and appreciation – extended to this task. Despite the challenges, fieldwork projects centered on the period are ongoing at Karphi (Wallace 2021) and the Porto Rafti bay (Murray & Lis 2023).

Major breakthroughs for the understanding of the period have been inspired by comparative approaches in adjacent disciplines, especially anthropology. Thus, the study of the LBA/EIA has become a dynamic arena impacting broader conversations in Greek and Mediterranean history and archaeology, on wide-ranging topics such as the collapse, demography, and burial (Sections 2, 4, and 7, respectively). Inspired by this, and by pleas for setting the period into interdisciplinary conversations (Knodell 2021: 244–5), I have focused on social change drawing from anthropological and sociological literature (Section 1). While acknowledging that "frustratingly little can be said with much certainty about the nature of social structure within the EIA communities" (Dickinson 2006: 252), I have discussed and critiqued a range of influential models and discourses developed in the scholarship of the last decades.

All in all, over a century of research (and especially the last half of it) has established that only if we integrate the production of new datasets, with new approaches and interdisciplinary conversations, can we effectively enrich, complicate, and transform our understanding of the end of the Aegean Bronze Age, and highlight its importance for the study of Greek, Mediterranean and other antiquity.

Appendix: Chronology

The relative chronology surrounding the end of the Bronze Age is characterized by a profusion of terms (see, e.g., Morris 2000: 79–88; Lemos 2002: 3–8; Dickinson 2006: 13–23; Kotsonas 2016). Inspired by cultural history, the term Mycenaean Palatial period is applied to the fourteeenth and thirteenth centuries, while Postpalatial encompasses the twelfth and partly the eleventh. However, this terminology underplays the fact that palatial authority affected directly only a fraction of the Aegean. Culture history also inspired the designation Dark Age(s), which was applied from the twelfth or eleventh to the tenth or eighth centuries, and colored negatively the study of the period (Morris 2000: 79–88; Kotsonas 2016). Despite arguments for its persisting popularity (Murray 2018a), the term has been largely superseded in specialized scholarship by the designation EIA, which is inspired by the three-age system of European Prehistory and is applied to the twelfth to seventh centuries (Kotsonas 2016). Chronological subdivisions within this timespan depend on ceramic styles and stratigraphic associations (e.g., Lemos 2002: 9–24; Deger-Jalkotzy & Bächle 2009; Moschos 2009). Accordingly, the LH/LM IIIC period is followed by the Submycenaean/ Subminoan (which may be a style, rather than a period; see Warren & Hankey 1989: 107–8; Lemos 2002: 7–8; Dickinson 2006: 14–6; Kotsonas 2008a: 32–3, 35–6), the Protogeometric, Geometric (or Subprotogeometric), and Orientalizing (or Subgeometric). This terminological range is indicative of a conceptual divide between the end of the 2nd millennium, which is articulated through reference to the past (cf. Postpalatial, or Submycenaean/Subminoan), and the early 1st millennium, which is labeled in forward-looking terms (Protogeometric leading to Geometric). Another problem lies in the treatment of the different pottery styles of the EIA as a neat "chest of drawers" (Papadopoulos 1997: 191. Cf. Crellin 2021: 6–7), the limitations of which were demonstrated, for example, by three major conferences on the chronology of the LH IIIC period (see e.g. Deger-Jalkotzy & Bächle 2009), and by a recent study which established that "Protogeometric" concentric circles can occur in the same layer as LH IIIC pottery (Van Damme & Lis 2024).

The absolute chronology of the end of the Bronze Age remained uncontested for too long (Figure 10) (Warren & Hankey 1989: 158–69; Lemos 2002: 23–6; Dickinson 2006: 20–3). The collapse of the Mycenaean palaces was placed ca.

TRADITIONAL CHRONOLOGIES		ABSOLUTE DATES	PROPOSED REVISIONS TO MAINLAND CHRONOLOGIES		
Crete	Mainland	Date BCE	Assiros	Sindos	Zagora
		1400			
LM IIIA1	LH IIIA1		LH IIIA2		
LM IIIA2	LH IIIA2		LH IIIB		
		1300			
	LH IIIB1		LH IIIC		
LM IIIB	LH IIIB2			EPG	
		1200/1190			
	LH IIIC-early		LH IIIC	?	
		1150/1140			
LM IIIC	LH IIIC-middle		?		
		1100/1090			
Central Cretan pottery sequence	LH IIIC-late & SubMyc		EPG	LPG	
SubMin	Attic pottery sequence	1025		EG	
	EPG & MPG			MG I	
		950			
EPG	LPG			MG II	MG
		900			
MPG	EG I & II				
LPG					
PGB	MG I	850		LG Ia	LG I
EG		800			
MG	MG II & LG Ia			LG Ib	
		750			
LG	LG Ib, II & IIb				
		700			

Figure 10 Traditional and revised chronologies of the Aegean at the end of the second and early 1st millennium.

1200 BCE based on ceramic cross-dating of Mycenaean pottery in Egypt and the Levant (Warren & Hankey 1989: 159–62; Jung & Kardamaki 2022). Historical dates were again available only in the eighth century, with the discovery of Greek Geometric pottery in destruction levels of Near Eastern cities dated on historical grounds, and in Italian and Sicilian sites reportedly colonized by Greeks on specific calendar years (e.g., Coldstream 1968: 302–31; 1977). The chronology of the period in between was approached through educated guesses based on notions of stylistic development and the quantity of material known from each ceramic sub-phase. Accordingly, the Postpalatial period, or IIIC phase, was largely identified with the twelfth century, while – when treated as distinct periods – the Submycenaean and Subminoan were taken to cover (part of) the eleventh century. In the mainland, the beginning of Protogeometric was placed in the eleventh century, and the phase was taken to cover the entire tenth century, while in Crete, Protogeometric stretched over the tenth and ninth centuries (Warren & Hankey 1989: 169; Lemos 2002: 23–6). In both areas, Geometric covered (part of) the ninth and eighth centuries, while Orientalizing/Subgeometric was applied to the seventh (Coldstream 1968: 302–31; 1977).

Although scholars acknowledged – and lamented – limitations over the absolute chronology of the period, little energy was invested in revising the evidential basis for it. A notable exception was provided by the radical revision of the Egyptian – and thus of the broader Eastern Mediterranean – traditional chronology in the *Centuries of Darkness* (James et al. 1991), which argued for compressing the "Dark Age" from five into two centuries. Very different, science-based revisions to the chronology of the Aegean in this period were proposed in the last two decades (Figure 10). The proposals in question rely, on the one hand, on dendrochronological and radiocarbon data from sites in central Macedonia, including Assiros and Sindos (Newton, Kuniholm, & Wardle 2005; Wardle, Higham, & Kromer 2014; Gimatzidis & Weninger 2020; Gimatzidis 2021); and, on the other hand, by radiocarbon results from nonGreek sites in the Mediterranean, from Sidon to Huelva, which favor a higher chronology for the Aegean EIA (van der Plicht, Bruins, & Nijboer 2009; Fantalkin, Finkelstein, & Piasetzky 2015; Mederos Martín 2020; Doumet-Serhal et al. 2023; López Castro et al. 2024: 378–84). These results were lately corroborated by radiocarbon data from Zagora on Andros, in the central Aegean (Alagich et al. 2024). However, not all new analyses question the traditional chronology. A project which targeted three major Aegean multi-period sites (Lefkandi, Kalapodi, Corinth), which are extensively explored and boast well-studied sequences that are fundamental to the traditional chronology of the EIA, reaffirmed the validity of the traditional chronology, at least for the Submycenaean period (Toffolo et al. 2013). The traditional chronology also received confirmation (for the most part) by results from the central Macedonian site of Kastanas (Weninger & Jung 2009) and from sites in Israel (Fantalkin, Finkelstein & Piasetzky 2015).

Notwithstanding the divisions between those who challenge and defend the traditional chronology, and the notable discrepancies between the different suggestions for revisions, the fluid state of the field can be summarized as follows: for the LBA and the beginning of the EIA, the analytical results obtained from central Macedonia are contrasting; those from Kastanas support the traditional chronology for the end of the LH IIIB to the Protogeometric period (Weninger & Jung 2009: esp. fig. 14) and agree with the data from Israel (Fantalkin, Finkelstein & Piasetzky 2015: esp. Table 3). On the contrary, the results from Assiros suggest that the absolute chronology of: LH IIIA should be raised by 30 to 50 years; LH IIIB should be raised by 40 to 80 years; LH IIIC should be raised by 100 to 150 years; and Early Protogeometric by ca. 100 years (Wardle, Higham & Kromer 2014: esp. Table 1). The results from Sindos and elsewhere in the Mediterranean cover only the Protogeometric and Geometric periods, and they recall the data from Assiros in favoring a considerably higher chronology. Indeed, these results suggest that the date of the Late Protogeometric and Early Geometric period should be raised by a century and a half, and be extended in length by one or more decades; Middle Geometric I and II should be raised by somewhat less, and be extended slightly (from 50 to 60 years); Late Geometric Ia should be raised from 760–750 BCE to 870–790 BCE, and thus be extended in length by eight times; and Late Geometric Ib should be raised from 750–735 BCE to 790–730 BCE, and thus be extended by four times (Gimatzidis & Weninger 2020: esp. fig. 11). The radiocarbon evidence from Zagora favors the raising the date of Middle Geometric by one or two centuries (with the lower figure applying to Middle Geometric II), and of Late Geometric I by one century (Alagich et al. 2024: esp. Table 2). Analytical results from elsewhere in the Mediterranean also favor the raising of the chronology of the Greek Geometric ceramic sequence, typically to a dissimilar extent, and sometimes to dates which are higher than those obtained from Aegean samples (van der Plicht, Bruins & Nijboer 2009; Mederos Martín 2020; Doumet-Serhal et al. 2023: fig. 36; López Castro et al. 2024: 378–84).

These results are intriguing; yet, most Aegeanists have barely engaged with them, let alone adopted them. One could perhaps blame this on inertia, but I think it is also because of some peculiarities in the approaches of the revisionist projects. First, these projects typically target sites located not in the core area of Greece (where most of the different pottery styles concerned were introduced), but in the fringes of the Aegean and well beyond it. The traditional chronology of the Aegean EIA depends on dates from elsewhere in the Mediterranean, but perpetuating this tradition irrespective of the methodological shift to scientific analyses is questionable. Radiocarbon and dendrochronological dating for different Mediterranean cultures is typically based on sampling of key sites within core areas of these cultures (e.g., Gordion for Phrygia: Rose & Darbyshire 2011). Second, although the revisionist projects make general claims about the Aegean EIA chronology, they are centered on the undeniably essential Attic (see, e.g., the focus of Gimatzidis & Weninger 2020 on Late Geometric Ia and Ib, which are exclusive to Attica, according to Coldstream 1968: 330) and Euboean chronologies; and yet, they refrain from sampling sites in these two regions. Third, the sampling of most of the revisionist projects targeting Aegean sites covers only animal bone from single trenches (Gimatzidis & Weninger 2020; Alagich et al. 2024). Fourth, the Aegean sites and deposits targeted span only part of the EIA and/or the transition from the Bronze Age, which leaves uncertainties over how these partial new sequences relate to well-established chronological lynch pins, such as the collapse of 1200 BCE. Fifth, instead of following the example of Anatolian archaeology, where the new chronology of the Phrygian EIA was established through the publication of an entire monograph dedicated to dendrochronological and radiocarbon data and their historical implications (Rose & Darbyshire 2011), the proposed revisions of Aegean chronology appear in brief articles that leave little space for historical contextualization. Sixth, the way in which some of the revisionist studies dismiss the data, methodologies, and interpretations of fellow researchers raises concerns about objectivity and reliability. Exploring alternative interpretations of inconsistent results, seeking common ground, and acknowledging regional variation would be more productive. Concerns over site and sample selection, developing methodologies, historical interpretation, and the constructive ways to debate it can be addressed more effectively through lessons learnt from the debate over the absolute chronology of EIA Israel (e.g., Fantalkin, Finkelstein & Piasetzky 2015; Finkelstein & Piasetzky, 2024).

Particularly promising for the field is the expansive and systematic project of radiocarbon analysis, which is currently being pursued on material from the Athenian Agora, a well-excavated, well-published, and thoroughly reviewed site, the primary data from which has long been fundamental to the chronology of the EIA and has been scrutinized by scholarship. John Papadopoulos (pers. comm.) highlights the methodological advantages presented by the Athenian Agora project, which samples human bone collagen from inhumation tombs, apatite from cremated human bone, and short-lived organic samples, especially seeds (as opposed to animal bones, which can come from deposits that are not demonstrably primary). Papadopoulos reports that the preliminary results of the project favor a modestly higher chronology, especially for the Protogeometric and Early Geometric periods. Additionally, the results of radiocarbon and thermoluminicense analyses of EIA material from the settlement of Thorikos is forthcoming (Roald Docter pers. comm.).

Clearly, more and better-quality data from different sites is needed before Aegeanists can agree on raising the absolute chronology of the EIA. Until a robust new scheme is better-grounded, I feel compelled to follow others in retaining the traditional chronology.

References

Alagich, R., Becerra-Valdivia, L., Miller, M. C., Trantalidou, K., and Smith, C. (2024). Mediterranean Early Iron Age chronology: Assessing radiocarbon dates from a stratified Geometric period deposit at Zagora (Andros), Greece. *Antiquity* **98**, 454–69.

Alexandridou, A. (2020). Athens and Attica. In I. S. Lemos and A. Kotsonas, eds., *A Companion to the Archaeology of Early Greece and the Mediterranean*. Hoboken, NJ: Wiley Blackwell, pp. 743–62.

Andreou, H. and Kleitsas, C. (2018). 1979–2009: Αρχαιολογικές έρευνες κοιλάδας ποταμού Γορμού Πωγωνίου Ιωαννίνων. *Το Αρχαιολογικό Έργο στη Βορειοδυτική Ελλάδα και τα Νησιά του Ιονίου* **1**, 87–100.

Andronikos, M. (1954). Η «δωρική εισβολή» και τα αρχαιολογικά ευρήματα. *Hellenika* **13**, 221–40.

Antonaccio, C. M. (1995). Homer and Lefkandi. In Ø. Andersen and M. Dickie, eds., *Homer's World: Fiction, Tradition, Reality* (Papers from the Norwegian Institute at Athens 3). Bergen: Åström, pp. 5–27.

Arrington, N. (2016). Talismanic practice at Lefkandi: Trinkets, burials and belief in the Early Iron Age. *The Cambridge Classical Journal* **62**, 1–30.

Aruz, J., Rakic, Y., and Graff, S., eds. (2014). *Assyria to Iberia at the Dawn of the Classical Age*. New Haven, CT: Yale University Press.

Bendall, L. M. (2007). *Economics of Religion in the Mycenaean World: Resources Dedicated to Religion in the Mycenaean Palace Economy* (School of Archaeology Monograph 67). Oxford: Oxford School of Archeology.

Bennet, J. (2007). The Aegean Bronze Age. In W. Scheidel, I. Morris, and R. P. Saller, eds., *The Cambridge Economic History of the Greco-Roman World*. Cambridge: Cambridge University Press, pp. 175–210.

Betancourt, P. P. (1976). The end of the Greek Bronze Age. *Antiquity* **50**, 40–7.

Bettelli, M. (2015). From wanax to basileus: Archaeological evidence of military and political leadership in Late Mycenaean society. *Origini: Preistoria e protostoria delle civiltà antiche* **38**, 123–50.

Bintliff, J. (2020). Natural and human ecology: Geography, climate, and demography. In I. S. Lemos and A. Kotsonas, eds., *A Companion to the Archaeology of Early Greece and the Mediterranean*. Hoboken, NJ: Wiley Blackwell, pp. 3–32.

Blackwell, N. G. (2018). Contextualizing Mycenaean hoards: Metal control on the Greek Mainland at the end of the Bronze Age. *AJA* **122**(4), 509–39.

Borgna, E. (2024). Hoards and hoarding from the Alps to the Aegean: A comparative view. In E. Borgna, ed., *Nature and Function of Bronze Deposition between Europe and the Mediterranean: Hoards of the Late Bronze Age* (West & East Monografie, 5). Trieste: Edizioni Università di Trieste, pp. 1–18.

Bourogiannis, G. (2018). The Phoenician presence in the Aegean during the Early Iron Age: Trade, settlement and cultural interaction. *RStFen* **46**, 43–88.

Bowers, M. (2025). *Continuity and Change in the Textile Culture of the Late Bronze Age and Early Iron Age Aegean*. Ph.D. dissertation. Macquarie University.

Brock, J. K. (1957). *Fortetsa: Early Greek Tombs near Knossos*. Cambridge: Cambridge University Press.

Broodbank, C. (2013). *The Making of the Middle Sea: A History of the Mediterranean from the Beginning to the Emergence of the Classical World*. London: Thames and Hudson.

Bulatović, A., Molloy, B., and Filipović, V. (2021). The Aegean migrations revisited: Changes in material culture and settlement patterns in the LBA in the Central Balkans in the light of new data. *Starinar* **71**, 61–105.

Bulmer, P. (2020). Continuities and changes in Mycenaean burial practices after the collapse of the palace system. In G. D. Middleton, ed., *Collapse and Transformation: The Late Bronze Age to Early Iron Age in the Aegean*. Oxford and Philadelphia: Oxbow Books, pp. 145–52.

Burkert, W. (1977). *Griechische Religion der archaischen und klassischen Epoche*. Stuttgart: Kohlhammer.

Carpenter, R. (1966). *Discontinuity in Greek Civilization*. Cambridge: Cambridge University Press.

Catling, R. W. V. (1998). The typology of the Protogeometric and Subprotogeometric pottery from Troia and its Aegean context. *Studia Troica* **8**, 151–87.

Catling, R. W. V. and Lemos, I. S. (1990). *Lefkandi II.1: The Protogeometric Building at Toumba. Part 1: The Pottery*. London: The British School of Archaeology at Athens/Thames & Hudson.

Cavanagh, W. and Mee, C. (1998). *A Private Place: Death in Prehistoric Greece*. Jonsered: Paul Åströms Förlag.

Cerasuolo, O., ed. (2021). *The Archaeology of Inequality: Tracing the Archaeological Record*. Albany: State University of New York Press.

Chadwick, J. (1976). Who were the Dorians? *PP* **31**, 103–17.

Charalambidou, X. (2025). The social roles of feasting in the central and southern Aegean from the Postpalatial to the Early Archaic period. In C. Morgan, J. P. Crielaard, and X. Charalambidou, eds., *Feasting with the*

Greeks: Towards a Social Archaeology of Ritual Consumption in the Greek World. Amsterdam: Amsterdam University Press.

Chase-Dunn, C. and Babones, S. J. (2006). Introduction. In *Global Social Change: Historical and Comparative Perspectives*. Baltimore: John Hopkins University Press, pp. 1–7.

Chase-Dunn, C. and Lerro, B. (2014). *Social Change: Globalization from the Stone Age to the Present*. Abingdon and New York: Routledge.

Chatzina, Y., Kardamaki, E., Kostoula, M., Maran, J., and Papadimitriou, A. (2023). I see friends shaking hands ... An early evidence for a long-lasting social gesture on a Mycenaean pictorial krater from Tiryns. In A. L. D'Agata and P. Pavúk, eds., *The Lady of Pottery: Ceramic Studies Presented to Penelope A. Mountjoy in Acknowledgement of Her Outstanding Scholarship* (SMEA n.s. supplement 3). Rome: Quasar, pp. 17–38.

Chemsseddoha, A. Z. (2019). *Les pratiques funéraires de l'âge du Fer en Grèce du Nord: étude d'histoires régionales*. Bordeaux: Ausonius Editions.

Cherry, J. (1988). Pastoralism and the role of animals in pre and protohistoric economies of the Aegean. In C. R. Whittaker, ed., *Pastoral Economies in Classical Antiquity* (Cambridge Philological Society Supplementary Volume 14), pp. 6–34, Cambridge: Cambridge Philological Society.

Christakopoulou-Somakou, O. G. (2009). *Το νεκροταφείο της Στάμνας και η Πρωτογεωμετρική περίοδος στην Αιτωλοακαρνανία*. Ph.D. dissertation. University of Athens.

Cline, E. H. (1994). *Sailing the Wine Dark Sea: International Trade and the Late Bronze Age Aegean* (BAR IS 591). Oxford: Tempus Reparatum.

Cline, E. H. (2021). *1177 B.C. The Year Civilization Collapsed*, 2nd ed. Princeton and Oxford: Princeton University Press.

Cline, E. H. (2024). *After 1177 B.C: The Survival of Civilizations*. Princeton and Oxford: Princeton University Press.

Coldstream, J. N. (1968). *Greek Geometric Pottery*. London: Methuen.

Coldstream, J. N. (1977). *Geometric Greece, 900–700 BC*. London: E. Benn.

Coldstream, J. N. and Catling, H. W., eds. (1996). *Knossos North Cemetery: Early Greek Tombs*, vol. I–IV (BSA Supplementary Volume 28). London: British School at Athens.

Cosmopoulos, M. B. (2014). Cult, continuity, and social memory: Mycenaean Eleusis and the transition to the Early Iron Age. *AJA* **118**(3), 401–27.

Cosmopoulos, M. B. (2019). State formation in Greece: Iklaina and the unification of Mycenaean Pylos. *AJA* **123**(3), 349–80.

Cosmopoulos, M. B. (2025). *The World of Homer: Archaeology, Social Memory, and the Emergence of Early Greek Epic Poetry*. Cambridge: Cambridge University Press.

Crellin, R. J. (2021). *Change and Archaeology*. London and New York: Routledge.

Crielaard, J. P. (2011). The "wanax to basileus" model reconsidered: Authority and ideology after the collapse of the Mycenaean palaces. In A. Mazarakis Ainian, ed., *The "Dark Ages" Revisited: Acts of an International Symposium in Memory of William D.E. Coulson, University of Thessaly, Volos, 14–17 June 2007*. Volos: University of Thessaly, pp. 83–111.

Crielaard, J. P. and Driessen, J. (1994). The hero's home: Some reflections on the building at Toumba, Lefkandi. *Topoi* **4**, 254–67.

D'Agata, A.-L. (2012). The power of images: A figured krater from Thronos Kephala (ancient Sybrita) and the process of polis formation in Early Iron Age Crete. *SMEA* **54**, 207–47.

Dakouri-Hild, A. (2005). Breaking the mould? Production and economy in the Theban state. In A. Dakouri-Hild and S. Sherratt, eds., *Autochthon: Papers Presented to O.T.P.K. Dickinson on the Occasion of his Retirement* (BAR IS 1432). Oxford: Archaeopress, pp. 207–41.

Dakouri-Hild, A. and Boyd, M. J., ed. (2016). *Staging Death: Funerary Performance, Architecture and Landscape in the Aegean*. Berlin: De Gruyter.

Day, P. M. and Kardamaki, E. (2025). Potting communities during the Mycenaean palatial period. In D. Pullen, ed., *Social Groups and Production in Mycenaean Economies. Papers from the Langford Conference, Florida State University, Tallahassee, 24–25 February 2023*. Leiden: Sidestone Press, pp. 141–72.

Day, L. P. and Snyder, L. M. (2004). The "big house" at Vronda and the "great house" at Karphi: Evidence for social structure in LM IIIC Crete. In L. P. Day, M. S. Mook, and J. P. Muhly, eds., *Crete beyond the Palaces: Proceedings of the Crete 2000 Conference* (Prehistory Monographs 10). Philadelphia, PA: INSTAP Academic Press, pp. 63–80.

Deger-Jalkotzy, S. (2006). Late Mycenaean warrior tombs. In S. Deger-Jalkotzy and I. S. Lemos, eds., *Ancient Greece: From the Mycenaean Palaces to the Age of Homer* (Edinburgh Leventis Studies 3). Edinburgh: Edinburgh University Press, pp. 151–79.

Deger-Jalkotzy, S. and Bächle, A. E., eds. (2009). *LH III C Chronology and Synchronisms III: LH III C Late and the Transition to the Early Iron Age. Proceedings of the International Workshop Held at the Austrian Academy of Sciences at Vienna, February 23rd and 24th, 2007*. Wien: Verlag der Österreichischen Akademie der Wissenschaft.

Deger-Jalkotzy, S. and Lemos, I. S., eds. (2006). *Ancient Greece from the Mycenaean Palaces to the Age of Homer*. Edinburgh: Edinburgh University Press, pp. 337–60.

De Polignac, F. (1984). *La naissance de la cité grecque*. Paris: La découverte.

Desborough, V. R. d'A. (1952). *Protogeometric Pottery*. Oxford: Clarendon Press.

Desborough, V. R. (1964). *The Last Mycenaeans and Their Successors*. Oxford: Clarendon Press.

Desborough, V. R. (1972). *The Greek Dark Ages*. Oxford: Benn.

Dibble, F. and Fallu, D. (2020). New data from old bones: A taphonomic reassessment of Early Iron Age beef ranching at Nichoria, Greece. *JAS: Reports* **30**(102234). https://doi.org/10.1016/j.jasrep.2020.102234.

Dibble, F. and Finné, M. (2021). Socioenvironmental change as a process: Changing foodways as adaptation to climate change in South Greece from the Late Bronze Age to the Early Iron Age. *Quaternary International* **597**, 50–62.

Dickinson, O. (2006). *The Aegean from Bronze Age to Iron Age: Continuity and Change between the Twelfth and Eighth Centuries BC*. London and New York: Routledge.

Dierckx, H. (1986). *The Dorian Dilemma: Problems and Interpretations of Social Change in Late Helladic III C and Dark Age Greece with Reference to the Archaeological and Literary Evidence*. MA dissertation. Durham University.

Diffey, C., Styring, A., Orengo, H. A. et al. (2025). Late Bronze – Early Iron Age Agro-systems in Northern Greece: New Insights through Stable Isotope Analysis from Methone, Pieria. *Environmental Archaeology* **30**(4). https://doi.org/10.1080/14614103.2025.2535768.

Di Lorenzo, G. (2023). Italic and Central European metals found in western Greece during the LHIIIC period: For a contextual approach. *ASAtene* **101**, 26–57.

Dimitriadou, E. M. (2019). *Early Athens: Settlements and Cemeteries in the Submycenaean, Geometric, and Archaic Periods*. Los Angeles: Cotsen Institute of Archaeology Press at UCLA.

Donnellan, L. (2017). The "Euboean" koine: Reassessing patterns of cross-cultural interaction and exchange in the north-western Aegean region. In S. Handberg and A. Gadolou, eds., *Material Koinai in the Greek Early Iron Age and Archaic Period: Acts of an International Conference at the Danish Institute at Athens, 30 January–1 February 2015* (Monographs of the Danish Institute at Athens, 22). Aarhus: Aarhus University Press, pp. 43–63.

Doumet-Serhal, C., Gimatzidis, S., Weninger, B., von Rüden C., and Kopetzky, K. (2023). An interdisciplinary approach to Iron Age Mediterranean chronology through combined archaeological and ^{14}C-radiometric evidence from Sidon, Lebanon. *PLoS ONE* **18**(3), e0274979. https://doi.org/10.1371/journal.pone.0274979.

Drews, R. (1993). *The End of the Bronze Age: Changes in Warfare and the Catastrophe ca. 1200 bc*. Princeton: Princeton University Press.

Duday, H. (2009). *The Archaeology of the Dead: Lectures in Archaeothanatology*. Oxford: Oxbow Books.

Duray, A. (2020). *The Idea of Greek (Pre)History: Archaeological Knowledge Production and the Making of "Early Greece," c. 1950–1980*. Ph.D. dissertation. Stanford University.

Eaby, M. (2007). *Mortuary Variability in Early Iron Age Cretan Burials*. Ph.D. dissertation. University of North Carolina at Chapel Hill.

Eder, B. (2019). The role of sanctuaries and the formation of Greek identities in the LBA/EIA transition. In I. S. Lemos and A. Tsingarida, eds., *Beyond the Polis: Rituals, Rites and Cults in Early and Archaic Greece (12th–6th Centuries BC)*. Brussels: CreA-Patrimoine, pp. 25–52.

Eder, B. and Jung, R. (2015). Unus pro omnibus, omnes pro uno: The Mycenaean palace system. In J. Weilhartner and F. Ruppenstein, eds., *Tradition and Innovation in the Mycenaean Palatial Polities: Proceedings of an International Symposium Held at the Austrian Academy of Sciences, Vienna, 1–2 March, 2013*. Vienna: Verlag der Österreichischen Akademie der Wissenschaften, pp. 113–40.

Eder, B. and Lemos, I. S. (2020). From the collapse of the Mycenaean palaces to the emergence of Early Iron Age communities. In I. S. Lemos and A. Kotsonas, eds., *A Companion to the Archaeology of Early Greece and the Mediterranean*. Hoboken, NJ: Wiley Blackwell, pp. 133–60.

Eshel, T., Gilboa, A., Yahalom-Mack, N., Tirosh, O., and Erel, Y. (2021). Debasement of silver throughout the Late Bronze – Iron Age transition in the Southern Levant: Analytical and cultural implications. *JAS* **125**, 1–26.

Evely, R. D. G. (2006). *Lefkandi IV: The Bronze Age: The Late Helladic IIIC Settlement at Xeropolis* (BSA Supplementary Volume 39). London: British School at Athens.

Fagerström, K. (1988). *Greek Iron Age Architecture: Developments through Changing Times*. Goteborg: Paul Åströms Förlag.

Fantalkin, A., Finkelstein, I., and Piasetzky, E. (2015). Late Helladic to Middle Geometric Aegean and contemporary Cypriot chronologies: A radiocarbon view from the Levant. *BASOR* **373**, 25–48.

Finkelstein, I. and Piasetzky, E. (2024). The Gezer discrepancy: Comments on recently published radiocarbon dates. *Journal of Eastern Mediterranean Archaeology and Heritage Studies* **12**(4), 437–43.

Finley, M. I. (1956). *The World of Odysseus*. London: Chatto.

Finley, M. I. (1957). The Mycenaean tablets and economic history. *The Economic History Review* **10**(1), 128–41.

Fischer, P. M. and Bürge, T., eds. (2017). *"Sea Peoples" Up-to-Date: New Research on Transformations in the Eastern Mediterranean in the 13th–11th Centuries BCE.* Vienna: Österreichische Akademie der Wissenschaften.

Foxhall, L. (1995). Bronze to iron: Agricultural systems and political structures in Late Bronze Age and Early Iron Age Greece. *BSA* **90**, 239–50.

Gaignerot-Driessen, F. (2014). Goddesses refusing to appear? Reconsidering the LM III Figures with Upraised Arms. *AJA* **118** (3), 489–520.

Galanakis, Y. (2020). Death and burial. In I. S. Lemos and A. Kotsonas, eds., *A Companion to the Archaeology of Early Greece and the Mediterranean.* Hoboken, NJ: Wiley Blackwell, pp. 349–74.

Galaty, M. and Parkinson, W. A. eds. (2007). *Rethinking Mycenaean Palaces*, 2nd ed. Los Angeles: Cotsen Institute of Archaeology.

Galaty, M. and Parkinson, W. A. (2025). Not a great kingdom: Mycenaean economic variation as a measure of nonintegration. In D. Pullen, ed., *Social Groups and Production in Mycenaean Economies. Papers from the Langford Conference, Florida State University, Tallahassee, 24–25 February 2023.* Leiden: Sidestone Press, pp. 47–58.

Giannopoulos, T. G. (2007). *Die letzte Elite der mykenischen Welt. Achaia in mykenischer Zeit und das Phänomen der Kriegerbestattungen im 12. – 11. Jahrhundert v. Chr.* Bonn: Rudolf Habelt.

Giannopoulos, T. G. (2025). Military technology at the end of the Aegean Bronze Age: The warrior burials of the north-western Peloponnese and their relation to the fall of the Mycenaean palaces. In *3rd International Conference on Ancient Greek and Byzantine Technology, Athens, 19–21 November 2024.*

Gilboa, A., Sharon, I., and Boaretto, E. (2008). Tel Dor and the chronology of Phoenician "pre- colonization" stages. In C. Sagona, ed., *Beyond the Homeland: Markers in Phoenician Chronology* (Ancient Near Eastern Studies Supplement 28). Louvain: Peeters, pp. 113–204.

Gilboa, A., Waiman-Barak, P., and Jones, R. (2015). On the origin of Iron Age Phoenician ceramics at Kommos, Crete: Regional and diachronic perspectives across the Bronze Age to Iron Age transition. *BASOR* **374**, 75–102.

Gimatzidis, S. (2021). Greek dates and chronologies revised: The historical and archaeological context of the radiocarbon dates from Sindos. In E. Kaiser and W. Schier, eds., *Time and Materiality: Periodization and Regional Chronologies at the Transition from Bronze to Iron Age in Eurasia (1200–600 BCE).* Rahden: Marie Leidorff, pp. 83–107.

Gimatzidis, S., ed. (2024). *Greek Iron Age Pottery in the Mediterranean World: Tracing Provenance and Socioeconomic Ties.* Cambridge: Cambridge University Press.

Gimatzidis, S. and Weninger, B. (2020). Radiocarbon dating the Greek Protogeometric and Geometric periods: The evidence of Sindos. *PLoS ONE* **15**, https://doi.org/10.1371/journal.pone.0232906.

Gonzáles de Canales, F., Llompart, J., and Montaño, A. (2024). Consumption of Geometric and Archaic Greek pottery in the emporion of Huelva (Tartessos, south-western Spain). In S. Gimatzidis, ed., *Greek Iron Age Pottery in the Mediterranean World: Tracing Provenance and Socioeconomic Ties*. Cambridge: Cambridge University Press, pp. 342–62.

Gounaris, A. P. (2002). Στοιχεία οικιστικής–πολεοδομίας–αρχιτεκτονικής των οικήσεων της Πρωτογεωμετρικής–Γεωμετρικής περιόδου και η συμβολή τους στην ερμηνεία γένεσης της πόλεως – Ηπειρωτική Ελλάς. Ph.D. dissertation. University of Crete.

Gounaris, A. P. (2007). Curvilinear versus rectangular? A contribution to the interpretation of the evolution in architectural forms in Greece during the Protogeometric–Geometric–Archaic periods based on a study of the constructions of Oropos. In A. Mazarakis Ainian, ed., *Oropos and Euboea in the Early Iron Age*. Volos: University of Thessaly, pp. 77–122.

Graeber, D. and Wengrow, D. (2021). *The Dawn of Everything: A New History of Humanity*. New York: Farrar, Straus and Giroux.

Graziadio, G. (2025). *The Aegean and Cyprus: Interaction between Two Distinct Cultural Mediterranean Areas from the Third Millennium to Ca 1200 BC*. Venice: Ca' Foscari.

Gürbüzer, M. (2022). The traces of the Early Iron Age at Amos. *TÜBA-AR Türkiye Bilimler Akademisi Arkeoloji Dergisi* **31**, 27–38.

Haggis, D. C. (1993). Intensive survey, traditional settlement patterns, and Dark Age Crete: The case of Early Iron Age Kavousi. *JMA* **6**, 131–74.

Haggis, D. C. (2013a). Destruction and the formation of static and dynamic settlement structures in the Aegean. In J. Driessen, ed., *Destruction: Archaeological, Philological and Historical Perspectives*. Louvain-la-Neuve: Presses universitaires de Louvain, pp. 63–87.

Haggis, D. C. (2013b). Social organization and aggregated settlement structure in an Archaic Greek city on Crete (ca 600 BC). In J. Birch, ed., *From Prehistoric Villages to Cities: Settlement Aggregation and Community Transformation*. New York: Routledge, pp. 63–86.

Hall, J. M. (1997). *Ethnic Identity in Greek Antiquity*. Cambridge: Cambridge University Press.

Hall, J. M. (2014). *A History of the Archaic Greek World, 1200–479 BCE*. 2nd ed. Chichester: Wiley Blackwell.

Halstead, P. (1992). The Mycenaean palatial economy: Making the most of the gaps in the evidence. *Proceedings of the Cambridge Philological Society* **38**, 57–86.

Halstead, P. (1999). Surplus and share-croppers: The grain production strategies of Mycenaean Palaces. In P. Betancourt, V. Karageorghis, R. Laffineur, and W.-D. Niemeier, eds., *Meletemata: Studies Presented to Malcolm H: Wiener as He Enters His 65th Year* (Aegaeum 20). Liège: Université de Liège, pp. 319–26.

Halstead, P. (2001). Mycenaean wheat, flax and sheep: Palatial intervention in farming and its implications for rural society. In S. Voutsaki and J. T. Killen, eds., *Economy and Politics in the Mycenaean Palace States* (Cambridge Philological Society Supplementary Volume 27). Cambridge: Cambridge Philological Society, pp. 38–50.

Hamilakis, Y. and Konsolaki, E. (2004). Pigs for the gods: Burnt animal sacrifices as embodied rituals at a Mycenaean sanctuary. *OJA* **23**(2), 135–51.

Harrell, K. (2014). Man/woman, warrior/maiden: The Lefkandi Toumba female burial reconsidered. In Y. Galanakis, T. Wilkinson, and J. Bennet, eds., *ΑΘΥΡΜΑΤΑ: Critical Essays on the Archaeology of the Eastern Mediterranean in Honour of E. Susan Sherratt*. Oxford: Archaeopress, pp. 99–104.

Hattler, C. ed. (2008). *Zeit der Helden: Die "dunklen Jahrhunderte" Griechenlands 1200–700 v.Chr. Katalog zur Ausstellung im Badischen Landesmuseum Schloss Karlsruhe*. Darmstadt: Primus – Badischen Landesmuseum Karlsruhe.

Hatzaki, E. and Kotsonas A. (2020). Knossos and north central Crete. In I. S. Lemos and A. Kotsonas, eds., *A Companion to the Archaeology of Early Greece and the Mediterranean*. Hoboken, NJ: Wiley Blackwell, pp. 1029–53.

Haysom, M. (2011). The strangeness of Crete: Problems for the protohistory of Greek religion. In M. Haysom and J. Wallensten, eds., *Current Approaches to Religion in Ancient Greece: Papers presented at a Symposium at the Swedish Institute at Athens, 17–19 April 2008, Stockholm*. Stockholm: Swedish Institute at Athens, pp. 95–110.

Haysom, M. (2019). Entangled religion, ritual and social practice: The case of Karphi. In I. S. Lemos and A. Tsingarida, eds., *Beyond the Polis: Rituals, Rites and Cults in Early and Archaic Greece (12th–6th Centuries BC)*. Brussels: CreA-Patrimoine, pp. 53–64.

Haysom, M. (2020). Religion and cult. In I. S. Lemos and A. Kotsonas, eds., *A Companion to the Archaeology of Early Greece and the Mediterranean*. Hoboken, NJ: Wiley Blackwell, pp. 317–48.

Haysom, M. (2024). Investigating the instability of religious material culture in Greek prehistory: The case of "bench shrines." In M. Haysom, M. Mili, and J. Wallenstein, eds., *The Stuff of the Gods: The Material Aspects of Religion in Ancient Greece*. Stockholm: Swedish Institutes at Athens and Rome, pp. 133–48.

Heyman, J. McC. (2005). Social change. *Encyclopedia of Anthropology, by James H. Birx*, 1st ed. Sage, *Credo Reference*, https://search.credoreference.com/articles/Qm9va0FydGljbGU6OTA2MjY2?aid=237298.

Hinojosa-Prieto, H. R. (2020). Estimation of the moment magnitude and local site effects of a postulated Late Bronze Age earthquake: Mycenaean citadels of Tiryns and Midea, Greece. *Annals of Geophysics* **63**(3), 1–27.

Hodos, T. (2020). *The Archaeology of the Mediterranean Iron Age: A Globalising World c.1000–600 BCE*. Cambridge, New York, Melbourne: Cambridge University Press.

Hölbl, G. (2015). Egyptian cultural values in the ancient Greek world during the Protogeometric to Archaic Periods. In M. L. Famà, I. Inferrera, and P. Militello, eds., *Magia d'Egitto: mostre archeologiche e convegni in Sicilia*. Palermo: Regione Siciliana, pp. 76–88.

Hooker, J. T. (1976). *Mycenaean Greece*. London: Routledge and Kegan Paul.

Horden, P. and Purcell, N. (2000). *The Corrupting Sea: A Study of Mediterranean History*. Malden: Blackwell.

Iakovidis, S. (1969–70). Περατή, το νεκροταφείον, Vols. A, and C. Athens: Library of the Archaeological Society.

Iezzi, C. (2009). Regional differences in the health status of the Mycenaean women of East Lokris. In L. A. Schepartz, S. C. Fox, and C. Bourbou, eds., *New Directions in the Skeletal Biology of Greece* (Hesperia Supplements 43). Princeton: American School of Classical Studies at Athens, pp. 175–92.

James, P. I., Thorpe, J., Kokkinos, N., Morkot, R., and Frankish, J. (1991). *Centuries of Darkness: A Challenge to the Chronology of Old World Archaeology*. London: Jonathan Cape.

Jantzen, U. (1972). *Samos VIII: Ägyptische und orientalische Bronzen aus dem Heraion von Samos*. Rudolf Habelt: Bonn.

Jazwa, K. (2019). Building change: Domestic architecture and identity during the Bronze Age to Iron Age transition. In P. Sapirstein and D. Scahill, eds., *New Directions and Paradigms for the Study of Greek Architecture*. Leiden: Brill, pp. 151–67.

Jung, R. (2002). *Kastanas: Ausgrabungen in Einem Siedlungshügel der Bronze- und Eisenzeit Makedoniens 1975–1979. Die Drehscheibenkeramik der Schichten 19 bis 11*. Kiel: Oetker.

Jung, R. (2017). Ταξικοί αγώνες και η πτώση των μυκηναϊκών ανακτόρων. *Κρίση* **1**(1), 78–126.

Jung, R. and Kardamaki, E. (2022). *Synchronizing the Destructions of the Mycenaean Palaces* (Mykenische Studien, 36; Denkschriften der philosophisch-historischen Klasse, 546). Vienna: Verlag der österreichischen Akademie der Wissenschaften.

Jung, R. and Mehofer, M. (2013). Mycenaean Greece and Bronze Age Italy: Cooperation, trade or war? *Archaeologisches Korrespondenzblatt* **43**, 175–93.

Kaklamani, O. (2021). *Το έθιμο της καύσης των νεκρών στα νησιά του Αιγαίου από την Πρωτογεωμετρική περίοδο έως και την Πρώιμη Αρχαϊκή Εποχή*. Ph.D. dissertation. University of Athens.

Kaniewski, D. and Van Campo, E. (2017). The climatic context of the 3.2 Kyr CalBP event. In P. M. Fischer and T. Bürge, eds., *"Sea Peoples" Up-to-Date: New Research on Transformations in the Eastern Mediterranean in the 13th–11th Centuries BCE*. Wien: Verlag der Österreichischen Akademie der Wissenschaften, pp. 85–94.

Kanta, A., Davaras, C., and Betancourt, P. P. (2022). *Honors to Eileithyia at Ancient Inatos: The Sacred Cave at Tsoutsouros, Crete*. Philadelphia: INSTAP Academic Press.

Karouzou, E. (2018). *Thessaly: From the Late Bronze Age to the Early Iron Age (1600-700 BC)*. Ph.D. dissertation. University of Oxford.

Kassianidou, V. (2023). Cypriot copper production, consumption and trade: Before and during the 12th century BC. In T. Bürge and P. M. Fischer, eds., *The Decline of Bronze Age Civilisations in the Mediterranean: Cyprus and Beyond* (SIMA 154). Nicosia: Astrom Editions, pp. 319–46.

Kelder, J. M. (2010). *The Kingdom of Mycenae: A Great Kingdom in the Late Bronze Aegean*. Bethesda, Md: CDL Press.

Killen, J. (1998). The rôle of the state in wheat and olive production in Mycenaean Crete. *Aevum* **72**(1), 19–23.

Killen, J. T. (2001). Some thoughts on ta-ra-si-ja. In S. Voutsaki and J. T. Killen, eds., *Economy and Politics in the Mycenaean Palace States* (Cambridge Philological Society Supplementary Volume 27). Cambridge: Cambridge Philological Society, pp. 161–80.

Killen, J. T. (2008). Mycenaean economy. In Y. Duhoux and A. Morpurgo Davies, eds., *A Companion to Linear B: Mycenaean Greek Texts and their World*, vol. 1. Louvain-la-Neuve: Peeters, pp. 159–200.

Kiderlen, M., Bode, M., Hauptmann, A., and Bassiakos, Y. (2016). Tripod cauldrons produced at Olympia give evidence for trade with copper from Faynan (Jordan) to south west Greece, c. 950–750 BCE. *JAS: Reports*, **8**, 303–13.

Kirk, G. S. (1990). *The Iliad: A Commentary*, Vol. II. Cambridge: Cambridge University Press.

Knapp, A. B. (2021). *Migration Myths and the End of the Bronze Age in the Eastern Mediterranean*. Cambridge: Cambridge University Press.

Knapp, A. B. and Manning, S. W. (2016). Crisis in context: The end of the Late Bronze Age in the Eastern Mediterranean. *AJA* **120**(1), 99–149.

Knodell, A. (2021). *Societies in Transition in Early Greece: An Archaeological History*. Oakland: University of California Press.

Kõiv, M. (2016). Communities and rulers in early Greece: Development of leadership patterns in Euboia and Argolis (12th–6th Centuries BC). In T. R. Kämmerer, M. Kõiv, and V. Sazonov, eds., *Kings, Gods and People: Establishing Monarchies in the Ancient World*. Münster: Ugarit-Verlag, pp. 293–354.

Konstantinidi-Syvridi, E. (2020). Jewelry. In I. S. Lemos and A. Kotsonas, eds., *A Companion to the Archaeology of Early Greece and the Mediterranean*. Hoboken, NJ: Wiley Blackwell, pp. 603–26.

Kotsonas, A. (2008a). *The Archaeology of Tomb A1K1 of Orthi Petra in Eleutherna: The Early Iron Age Pottery*. Athens: Publications of the University of Crete.

Kotsonas, A. (2008b). Review of O. Dickinson. 2006. The Aegean from Bronze Age to Iron Age: Continuity and Change between the Twelfth and Eighth Centuries BC. London and New York: Routledge. *CR* **58**(1), 255–6.

Kotsonas, A. (2009). Central Greece and Crete in the Early Iron Age. In A. Mazarakis Ainian, ed., *Proceedings of the International Conference 2º Αρχαιολογικό Έργο Θεσσαλίας και Στερεάς Ελλάδας 2003–2005*. Volos: University of Thessaly, pp. 1051–65.

Kotsonas, A. (2011). Review of S. Wallace. 2010. Ancient Crete: From Successful Collapse to Democracy's Alternatives, Twelfth to Fifth Centuries B.C. Cambridge and New York: Cambridge University Press. *BMCR 2011*, **4.52**.

Kotsonas A. (2012). Η ενεπίγραφη κεραμική του "Υπογείου": Προέλευση, τυπολογία, χρονολόγηση και ερμηνεία. In M. Bessios, Y. Tzifopoulos, and A. Kotsonas, eds., *ΜΕΘΩΝΗ ΠΙΕΡΙΑΣ Ι: Επιγραφές, χαράγματα και εμπορικά σύμβολα στη Γεωμετρική και Αρχαϊκή κεραμική από το 'Υπόγειο' της Μεθώνης Πιερίας στη Μακεδονία*. Thessaloniki: Center for the Greek Language, pp. 113–304.

Kotsonas, A. (2016). Politics of periodization and the archaeology of early Greece. *AJA* **120**(2), 239–70.

Kotsonas, A. (2017). Sanctuaries, temples and altars in the Early Iron Age: A chronological and regional accounting. In A. Mazarakis Ainian,

A. Alexandridou, and X. Charalambidou, eds., *Regional Stories towards a New Perception of the Early Greek World: An International Symposium in Honour of Professor Jan Bouzek, Volos, 18–21 June 2015*. Volos: University of Thessaly, pp. 55–66.

Kotsonas, A. (2018). Homer, the archaeology of Crete and the "tomb of Meriones" at Knossos. *JHS* **138**, 1–35.

Kotsonas, A. (2019). Early Iron Age Knossos and the development of the city of the historical period. In Κ. Μιτσοτάκη and Λ. Τζεδάκη-Αποστολάκη, eds., *Proceedings of the 12th International Cretological Conference*. Heraklion: Society of Cretan Historical Studies – Historical Museum of Crete, pp. 1–13. https://12iccs.proceedings.gr/en/proceedings/category/39/35/811.

Kotsonas, A. (2020). History of research. In I. S. Lemos and A. Kotsonas, eds., *A Companion to the Archaeology of Early Greece and the Mediterranean*. Hoboken, NJ: Wiley Blackwell, pp. 75–96.

Kotsonas, A. (2021). Making Cretan cities: Urbanisation, demography, and economies of production in the Early Iron Age and the Archaic period. In M. Gleba, B. Marín-Aguilera, and B. Dimova, eds., *Making Cities: Economies of Production and Urbanization in Mediterranean Europe, 1000–500 bc*. Cambridge: Macdonald Institute, pp. 57–76.

Kotsonas, A. (2023). New Mediterranean panoramas and their casts. *JMA* **36** (2), 237–41.

Kotsonas, A. (2024). *The Sanctuary of Hermes and Aphrodite at Syme Viannou VII: The Greek and Roman Pottery*. Athens and New York: Archaeological Society at Athens and New York University Press.

Kountouri, E. & A. Gadolou. (2019). *Σωστικές ανασκαφές της Αρχαιολογικής Υπηρεσίας. Ι, Τα νεκροταφεία, χωροταξική οργάνωση, ταφικά έθιμα, τελετουργίες*. Athens: ΤΑΠΑ.

Kourou, N. (2003). Des petits habitats de l'époque mycénienne à la cité-état d'époque historique. In M. Redde, L. Dubois, D. Briquel, H. Lavagne, and Fr. Queyrel, eds., *La naissance de la ville dans l'antiquite*. Paris: de Boccard, pp. 71–90.

Kourou, N. (2015). Cypriots and Levantines in the Central Aegean during the Geometric period: The nature of contacts. In J.-P. Descoeudres and S. Paspalas, eds., *Zagora in Context: Settlements and Intercommunal Links in the Geometric Period (900–700 BC), Proceedings of the Conference Held by the Australian Archaeological Institute at Athens and the Archaeological Society at Athens, Athens, 20–22 May, 2012* (*Mediterranean Archaeology* 25). Sydney: The University of Sydney, pp. 215–27.

Kourou, N. (2019). Phoenicians and Attic Middle Geometric pottery in the Mediterranean: Echoes of an early Athenian cultural value. In L. Bonadies,

I. Chirpanlieva, and É. Guillon, eds., *Les Phéniciens, les Puniques et les autres. Échanges et identités en Méditerranée ancienne* (Orient & Méditerranée 31). Paris: De Boccard, 159–77.

Kramer-Hajos, M. (2016). *Mycenaean Greece and the Aegean: Palace and Province in the Late Bronze Age.* Cambridge: Cambridge University Press.

Kurtz, D. C. and Boardman, J. (1971). *Greek Burial Customs.* London: Thames and Hudson.

Kyrieleis, H. (2006). *Olympische Forschungen 31: Anfänge und Frühzeit des Heiligtums von Olympia: Die Ausgrabungen am Pelopion 1987–1996.* Berlin and New York: Walter De Gruyter.

Langdon, S. ed. (1993). *From Pasture to Polis: Art in the Age of Homer.* Columbia and London: University of Missouri Press.

Langdon, S. (2015). Geometric pottery for beginners: Children and production in early Greece. In V. Vlachou, ed., *Pots, Workshops and Early Iron Age Society: Function and Role of Ceramics in Early Greece.* Brussels: CReA-Patrimoine, pp. 21–36.

Lebessi, A. (2002). *Το ιερό του Ερμή και της Αφροδίτης στη Σύμη Βιάννου III. Τα χάλκινα ανθρωπόμορφα ειδώλια.* Athens: Archaeological Society at Athens.

Lemos, I. S. (2002). *The Protogeometric Aegean.* Oxford: Oxford University Press.

Lemos, I. S. (2005). From palace to polis. Review of Thomas C. G. and C. Conant, eds., 1999. Citadel to City-State. The Transformation of Greece, 1200–700 B.C.E. Bloomington and Indianapolis: Indiana University Press. *The Classical Review* **55**(2), 569–70.

Lemos I. S. (2006). A new figurine from Xeropolis of Lefkandi. In E. Herring, I. Lemos, F. Lo Schiavo et al., eds., *Across Frontiers: Etruscans, Greeks, Phoenicians and Cypriots, Studies in honor of David Ridgway and Francesca Romana Serra Ridgway.* London: University of London, pp. 89–94.

Lemos, I. S. (2012). Euboea and Central Greece in the post palatial and early Greek periods. *AR* **58**, 19–27.

Lemos, I. (2014). Communities in transformation: An archaeological survey from the 12th to the 9th century BC. *Pharos* **20**(1), 161–92.

Lemos, I. S. (2022). Early Iron Age economies. In S. von Reden, ed., *The Cambridge Companion to the Ancient Greek Economy.* Cambridge: Cambridge University Press, pp. 15–28.

Lemos, I. S. and Kotsonas, A., eds. (2020). *A Companion to the Archaeology of Early Greece and the Mediterranean.* Hoboken, NJ: Wiley Blackwell.

Lemos, I. S., Livieratou, A., and Thomatos, M. (2009). Post-palatial urbanization: Some lost opportunities. In S. Owen and L. Preston, eds., *Inside the City in the Greek World.* Oxford: Oxbow Books, pp. 62–84.

Lemos, I. S. and Tsingarida, A., eds. (2019). *Beyond the Polis: Rituals, Rites and Cults in Early and Archaic Greece (12th–6th Centuries BC)*. Brussels: CreA-Patrimoine.

Lewartowski, K. (2000). *Late Helladic Simple Graves: A Study of Mycenaean Burial Customs* (BAR IS 878). Oxford: Archaeopress.

Lis, B. and Van Damme, T. (2021). Preliminary report on the Late Bronze Age pottery from ancient Eleon. *Mouseion* **18**, 48–85.

Lis, B., Mommsen, H. and Sterba, J. H. (2023). Production and distribution of White Ware towards the end of Late Bronze Age in Greece, *JAS: Reports* 47, https://doi.org/10.1016/j.jasrep.2022.103812.

López Castro, J. L., Jerbania, I. B., Mederos Martín, A., Martínez Hahnmüller, V., and Ferjaoui, A. (2024). Greek Geometric ceramics from Phoenician Utica: The closed context of Well 20017. In S. Gimatzidis, ed., *Greek Iron Age Pottery in the Mediterranean World: Tracing Provenance and Socioeconomic Ties*. Cambridge: Cambridge University Press, pp. 363–97.

Lupack, S. (2011). Redistribution in Aegean palatial societies. A view from outside the palace: The sanctuary and the damos in Mycenaean economy and society. *AJA* **115**(2), 207–17.

Lupack, S. (2020). Continuity and change in religious practice from the Late Bronze to the Iron Age. In G. D. Middleton, ed., *Collapse and Transformation: The Late Bronze Age to Early Iron Age in the Aegean*. Oxford and Philadelphia: Oxbow Books, pp. 161–7.

Mair, L. (1969). *Anthropology and Social Change*. London: The Athlone Press.

Mandalaki, S. (2006). Μάλια, Θέση Πεζούλα, (οικόπεδο Μιχαλάκη). *ADelt* **61** B2, 1134–7.

Manning, S. W., Kocik, C., Lorentzen, B., and Sparks, J. P. (2023). Severe multi-year drought coincident with Hittite collapse around 1198–1196 BC. *Nature* **614**, 719–24.

Marakas, G. (2010). *Ritual Practice between the Late Bronze Age and Protogeometric Periods of Greece* (BAR IS 2145). Oxford: Archaeopress.

Maran, J. (2000). Das Megaron im Megaron. Zur Datierung und Funktion des Antenbaus im mykenischen Palast von Tiryns. *AA*, 1–16.

Maran, J. (2012). Architektonischer Raum und soziale Kommunikation auf der Oberburg von Tiryns – Der Wandel von der mykenischen Palastzeit zur Nachpalastzeit. In F. Arnold, A. Busch, R. Haensch, and U. Wulf-Rheidt, eds., *Orte der Herrschaft: Charakteristika von antiken Machtzentren* (Menschen – Kulturen – Traditionen 3). Rahden: Marie Leidorf, pp. 149–62.

Maran, J. (2016). Against the currents of history: The early 12th-Century BCE resurgence of Tiryns. In J. Driessen, ed., *RA-PI-NE-U. Studies on the*

Mycenaean World Offered to Robert Laffineur for his 70th Birthday (Aegis 10). Louvain-la-Neuve: Presses universitaires de Louvain, pp. 201–20.

Maran, J. (2022). The demise of the Mycenaean palaces: The need for an interpretative reset. In R. Jung and E. Kardamaki, eds., *Synchronizing the Destructions of the Mycenaean Palaces* (Mykenische Studien, 36; Denkschriften der philosophisch-historischen Klasse, 546). Vienna: Verlag der österreichischen Akademie der Wissenschaften, pp. 231–53.

Maran, J. (2025). The Mycenae megaron ruin as a possible focus of social memory. In G. Shelach-Lavi, J. Maran and U. Davidovich, eds., *Rituals, Memory and Societal Dynamics: Contributions to Social Archaeology. A Collection of Essays in Memory of Sharon Zuckerman*. Turnhout: Brepols, pp. 51–75.

Maran, J. and Papadimitriou, A. (2006). Forschungen im Stadtgebiet von Tiryns 1999–2002. *AA*, 97–169.

Maran, J. and Papadimitriou, A. (2020). Mycenae and the Argolid. In I. S. Lemos and A. Kotsonas, eds., *A Companion to the Archaeology of Early Greece and the Mediterranean*. Hoboken, NJ: Wiley Blackwell, pp. 693–718.

Maran, J. and Wright, J.C. (2020). The rise of the Mycenaean culture, palatial administration and its collapse. In I. S. Lemos and A. Kotsonas, eds., *A Companion to the Archaeology of Early Greece and the Mediterranean*. Hoboken, NJ: Wiley Blackwell, pp. 99–132.

Masetti-Rouault, M. G., Calini, I., Hawley, R., and d'Alfonso, L., eds. (2024). *Ancient Western Asia beyond the Paradigm of Collapse and Regeneration (1200–900 BCE): Proceedings of the NYU-PSL International Colloquium, Paris Institut National d'Histoire de l'Art, April 16–17, 2019*. New York: New York University Press.

Matthäus, H. and Vonhoff, C. (2020). Bronze vessels. In I. S. Lemos and A. Kotsonas, eds., *A Companion to the Archaeology of Early Greece and the Mediterranean*. Hoboken, NJ: Wiley Blackwell, pp. 471–97.

Mazarakis Ainian, A. (1997). *From Rulers' Dwellings to Temples: Architecture, Religion and Society in Early Iron Age Greece (1100–700 B.C.)* (SIMA 121). Jonsered: Paul Åströms Förlag.

Mazarakis Ainian, A. (2001). From huts to houses in Early Iron Age Greece. In J. R. Brand and L. Karlsson, eds., *From Huts to Houses: Transformations of Ancient Societies. Proceedings of an International Seminar Organized by the Norwegian and Swedish Institutes in Rome, 21–24 September 1997*. Stockholm: Paul Åström Förlag, pp. 139–61.

Mazarakos, T., Tsatsaki, A., Litsa, M., and Tsaravopoulos, A. (2008). A Geometric location in Piraeus. In V. Sirbu and R. Stefanescu, eds., *Funerary Practices in Central and Eastern Europe (10th c. BC–3rd c. AD):*

Proceedings of the 10th International Colloquium of Funerary Archaeology. Tulcea (Dobruja–Romania), 10th–12th of October, 2008. Braila: Istros, Muzeul Brăilei, pp. 153–64.

McDonald, W. A., Coulson, W., and Rosser, J. (1983). *Excavations at Nichoria in Southwest Greece, Vol. 3: Dark Age and Byzantine occupation Minnesota Messenia Expedition*. Minneapolis: University of Minnesota Press.

Mederos Martín, A. (2020). La cronología absoluta del Protogeométrico y Geométrico griego y su impacto en los inicios de la colonización fenicia. In J. L. López Castro, ed., *Entre Utica y Gadir: navegación y colonización fenicia en el Mediterráneo Occidental a comienzos del I Milenio AC*. Granada: Comares, pp. 475–552.

Megaloudi, S. (2006). *Plants and Diet in Greece from Neolithic to Classic Periods: The Archaeobotanical Remains* (BAR IS 1516). Oxford: British Archaeological Reports.

Meiri, M., Stockhammer, P. W., Morgenstern, P., and Maran, J. (2019). Mobility and trade in Mediterranean antiquity: Evidence for an "Italian connection" in Mycenaean Greece revealed by ancient DNA of livestock. *JAS: Reports* **23**, 98–103.

Middleton, G. D. (2010). *The Collapse of Palatial Society in LBA Greece and the Postpalatial Period*. Oxford: Archaeopress.

Middleton, G. D. (2020). Mycenaean collapse(s) *c.* 1200 BC. In G. D. Middleton, ed., *Collapse and Transformation: The Late Bronze Age to Early Iron Age in the Aegean*. Oxbow Books: Philadelphia, pp. 9–22.

Millek, J. (2023). *Destruction and Its Impact on Ancient Societies at the End of the Bronze Age*. Columbus, GA: Lockwood Press.

Mina, M., Triantaphyllou, S., and Papadatos, Y. eds. (2016). *An Archaeology of Prehistoric Bodies and Embodied Identities in the Eastern Mediterranean*. Oxford and Philadelphia: Oxbow Books.

Mokrišová, J. and Verčík, M. (2022). Tradition and innovation in Aegean iron technologies: A view from Early Iron Age Ionia. *BSA* **117**, 137–68.

Molloy, B. (2023). Was there a 3.2 ka crisis in Europe? A critical comparison of climatic, environmental, and archaeological evidence for radical change during the Bronze Age–Iron Age transition. *JAR* **31**, 331–94.

Moore, W. E. (1963). *Social Change*. Englewood Cliffs, NJ: Prentice-Hall.

Morgan, C. (1999). *Isthmia VIII: The Late Bronze Age Settlement and Early Iron Age Sanctuary*. Princeton, NJ: American School of Classical Studies at Athens.

Morgan, C. (2024). Adding buildings to Early Iron Age sanctuaries: The materiality of built space. In M. Haysom, M. Mili, and J. Wallensten, eds., *The Stuff of the Gods: The Material Aspects of Religion in Ancient Greece*. Stockholm: Swedish Institutes at Athens and Rome, pp. 149–66.

Morris, I. (1987). *Burial and Ancient Society: The Rise of the Greek City State*. Cambridge: Cambridge University Press.

Morris, I. (1997). Homer and the Iron Age. In I. Morris and B. Powell, eds., *A New Companion to Homer*. Leiden: Brill, pp. 535–59.

Morris, I. (2000). *Archaeology as Cultural History*. Malden and Oxford: Blackwell.

Morris, I. (2007). Early Iron Age Greece. In W. Scheidel, I. Morris, and R. Saller, eds., *The Cambridge Economic History of the Greco Roman World*. Cambridge: Cambridge University Press, pp. 211–41.

Moschos, I. (2009). Evidence of social re-organization and reconstruction in Late Helladic IIIC Achaea and modes of contacts and exchange via the Ionian and Adriatic Sea. In E. Borgna and P. Cassola Guida, eds., *From the Aegean to the Adriatic: Social Organisations, Modes of Exchange and Interaction in Postpalatial Times (12th–11th B.C.)* (Studi e ricerche di protostoria mediterranea 8). Rome: Quasar, pp. 345–414.

Mountjoy, P. A. (2009). LH IIIC Late: An east Mainland-Aegean koine. In S. Deger-Jalkotzy and A. E. Bächle, eds., *LH III C Chronology and Synchronisms III: LH III C Late and the Transition to the Early Iron Age. Proceedings of the international workshop held at the Austrian Academy of Sciences at Vienna, February 23rd and 24th, 2007*. Wien: Verlag der Österreichischen Akademie der Wissenschaft, pp. 289–312.

Mountjoy, P. A. (2018). *Decorated Pottery in Cyprus and Philistia in the 12th Century BC, Cypriot IIIC and Philistine IIIC, Volumes I–II* (Contributions to the Chronology of the Eastern Mediterranean 36). Vienna: Verlag der Österreichischen Akademie der Wissenschaften.

Moutafi, I. (2021). *Towards a Social Bioarchaeology of the Mycenaean Period: A Biocultural Analysis of Human Remains from the Voudeni Cemetery, Achaea, Greece*. Oxford –Philadelphia: Oxbow Books.

Mühlenbruch, T. (2013). *Tiryns XVII.2: Baubefunde und Stratigraphie der Unterburgund des nordwestlichen Stadtgebiets (Kampagnen 1976 bis 1983): Die mykenische Nachpalastzeit (SH IIIC)*. Wiesbaden: Reichert.

Murray, S. C. (2017). *The Collapse of the Mycenaean Economy: Imports, Trade and Institutions 1300–700 BCE*. Cambridge: Cambridge University Press.

Murray, S. C. (2018a). Lights and darks: Data, labeling, and language in the history of scholarship on early Greece. *Hesperia* **87**(1), 17–54.

Murray, S. C. (2018b). Imported exotica and mortuary ritual at Perati in Late Helladic IIIC east Attica. *AJA* **122**(1), 33–64.

Murray, S. C. (2022). *Male Nudity in the Greek Iron Age: Representation and Ritual Context in Aegean Societies*. Cambridge and New York: Cambridge University Press.

Murray, S. C. (2023a). *Long-Distance Exchange and Inter-regional Economies.* (Cambridge Elements: Elements in the Aegean Bronze Age). Cambridge and New York: Cambridge University Press.

Murray, S. C. (2023b). Eastern Mediterranean Bronze Age trade in archaeological perspective: A review of interpretative and empirical developments. *Journal of Archaeological Research* **31**, 395–447.

Murray, S. C., Chorghay, I., and MacPherson, J. (2020). The Dipylon Mistress: Social and economic complexity, the gendering of craft production, and early Greek ceramic material culture. *AJA* **124**(2), 215–44.

Murray, S. C. and Lis, B. (2023). Documenting a maritime mercantile community through surface survey: Porto Rafti Bay in the post-collapse Aegean. *Antiquity* **97**(393), 1–7.

Mylonas, G. E. (1966). *Mycenae and the Mycenaean Age.* Princeton, NJ: Princeton University Press.

Nakassis, D. (2020). The economy. In I. S. Lemos and A. Kotsonas, eds., *A Companion to the Archaeology of Early Greece and the Mediterranean.* Hoboken, NJ: Wiley Blackwell, pp. 271–91.

Nakassis, D. (2025). Reading between the lines: Textual evidence for socio-economic organization in the Late Bronze Age. In D. Pullen, ed., *Social Groups and Production in Mycenaean Economies. Papers from the Langford Conference, Florida State University, Tallahassee, 24–25 February 2023.* Leiden: Sidestone Press, pp. 21–29.

Newton, M. W., Kuniholm, P. I., and Wardle, K. A. (2005). A dendrochronological 14 C wiggle-match for the Early Iron Age of North Greece. In T. E Levy and T. Higham, eds., *The Bible and Radiocarbon Dating: Archaeology, Text and Science.* London: Equinox. pp. 104–13.

Niemeier, W.-D. (2016). *Das Orakelheiligtum des Apollon von Abai/Kalapodi: Eines der bedeutendsten griechischen Heiligtümer nach den Ergebnissen der neuen Ausgrabungen* (Trierer Winckelmannsprogramme 25). Wiesbaden: Harrassowitz.

Nilsson, M. P. (1927). *The Minoan-Mycenaean Religion and Its Survival in Greek Religion.* Lund: C. W. K. Gleerup.

Noble, T., ed. (2000). *Social Theory and Social Change.* New York: St Martin's Press.

Norstein, F. E. and Selsvold, I., eds. (2025). *Archaeological Perspectives on Burial Practices and Societal Change: Death in Transition.* London: Routledge.

Nosch, M.-L. (2000). *The Organization of the Mycenaean Textile Industry.* Ph.D. dissertation. University of Salzburg.

Nowicki, K. (2000). *Defensible Sites in Crete c.1200–800 BC*. Liège: Université de Liège.

Nowicki, K. (2025). *Settlement in Crete during the Bronze to Iron Age Transition: The Crisis, Collapse and Reconstruction, ca. 1230–900 BC*. Berlin: de Gruyter.

Nur, A. and Cline, E. H. (2000). Poseidon's horses: Plate, tectonics and earthquake storms in the Late Bronze Age in the Aegean and eastern Mediterranean. *JAS* **27**, 43–63.

O'Brien, S. (2013). Parables of decline: Popular fears and the use of crises in Aegean archaeological interpretation. In E. M. van der Wilt, J. Martínez Jiménez, and G. Petruccioli, eds., *Tough Times: The Archaeology of Crisis and Recovery: Proceedings of the Graduate Archaeology at Oxford Conferences in 2010 and 2011*. Oxford: BAR, pp. 13–22.

Olsen, B. (2020). The people. In I. S. Lemos and A. Kotsonas, eds., *A Companion to the Archaeology of Early Greece and the Mediterranean*. Hoboken, NJ: Wiley Blackwell, pp. 293–316.

Paizi, P. (forthcoming). *Egyptian and Near Eastern Divinities in the Aegean of the Early Iron Age*. Ph.D. dissertation. University of Gratz.

Palermo, J. (2023). The development of ironworking in the 12th and 11th centuries in Cyprus. In T. Wilkinson and E. Sherratt, eds., *Circuits of Metal Value: Changing Roles of Metals in the Early Aegean and nearby Lands*. Oxford: Oxbow, pp. 116–44.

Palmer, R. (2001). Bridging the gap: The continuity of Greek agriculture from the Mycenaean to the historical period. In D. Tandy, ed., *Prehistory and History: Ethnicity, Class, and Political Economy*. Montreal: Black Rose Books, pp. 41–84.

Panagiotopoulou, E., Montgomery, J., Nowell, G. et al. (2018a). Detecting mobility in Early Iron Age Thessaly by Strontium Isotope Analysis. *EJA* **21**(4), 1–22.

Panagiotopoulou, E., van der Plicht, J., Papathanasiou, A. et al. (2018b). Diet and social divisions in protohistoric Greece. *JMA* **3**, 95–114.

Papadopoulos, J. K. (1993). To kill a cemetery: The Athenian Kerameikos and the Early Iron Age in the Aegean. *JMA* **6**, 175–206.

Papadopoulos, J. K. (1997). Phantom Euboians. *JMA* **10**(2), 191–219.

Papadopoulos, J. K. (2003). *Ceramicus Redivivus: The Early Iron Age Potters' Field in the Area of the Classical Athenian Agora* (Hesperia Supplement 31). Princeton, NJ: American School of Classical Studies at Athens.

Papadopoulos, J. K. (2005). *The Early Iron Age Cemetery at Torone*. Los Angeles: Cotsen Institute of Archaeology.

Papadopoulos, J. K. (2011). "Phantom Euboians" – A decade on. In D. Rupp and J. Tomlinson, eds., *Euboea and Athens: Proceedings of a Colloquium in Memory of Malcolm B. Wallace*, Athens: Canadian Institute in Greece, pp. 113–33.

Papadopoulou, A. (2017). Demographic properties in Early Iron Age and Early Archaic Aegean and the Mediterranean: The case of northern Greece. In A. Mazarakis Ainian, A. Alexandridou, and X. Charalambidou, eds., *Regional Stories towards a New Perception of the Early Greek World: An International Symposium in Honour of Professor Jan Bouzek, Volos, 18–21 June 2015*. Volos: University of Thessaly, pp. 605–31.

Papadopoulos, J. K. and Smithson, E. L. (2017). *The Athenian Agora 36: The Early Iron Age: The Cemeteries*. Princeton, NJ: American School of Classical Studies at Athens.

Papapostolou, I. A. (2008). *ΘΕΡΜΟΣ. Το Μέγαρο Β και το πρώιμο ιερό. Η ανασκαφή 1992–2003*. Athens: Archaeological Society at Athens.

Papathanasiou, A. and Richards, M. P. (2015). Summary: Patterns in the carbon and nitrogen isotope data through time. In A. Papathanasiou, M. P. Richards, and S. C. Fox, eds., *Archaeodiet in the Greek World: Dietary Reconstruction from Stable Isotope Analysis* (Hesperia Supplement 49). Princeton, NJ: American School of Classical Studies at Athens, pp. 195–204.

Pappi, E. (2014). *Ταφικές πρακτικές της Γεωμετρικής εποχής στο Άργος*. Ph.D. dissertation. University of Athens.

Pare, C. (2025). *Iron and the Iron Age: The Introduction of Iron in Europe and Western Asia*. Bicester: Archaeopress.

Parkinson, W. A. and Pullen, D. J. (2014). The emergence of craft specialization on the Greek Mainland. In D. Nakassis, J. Gulizio, and S. James, eds., *KE-RAME-JA: Studies Presented to Cynthia W. Shelmerdine*. Philadelphia, PA: INSTAP Academic Press, pp. 73–81.

Philippa-Touchais, A. (2011). "Cycles of collapse in Greek prehistory": Reassessing social change at the beginning of the Middle Helladic and the Early Iron Age. In A. Mazarakis Ainian, ed., *The "Dark Ages" Revisited: Acts of an International Symposium in Memory of W. D E. Coulson*. Volos: University of Thessaly, pp. 31–44.

Pierattini, A. (2022a). *The Origins of Greek Temple Architecture*. Cambridge: Cambridge University Press.

Pierattini, A. (2022b). The Toumba Building at Lefkandi: Preliminary Results of a New Architectural Analysis, colloquium organized at the University of Notre Dame.

Pollard, D. (2023). The history of settlement in Late Bronze Age and Early Iron Age Crete: A review and synthesis. *JGA* **8**, 104–46.

Pollard, D. and Whitelaw, T. (2025). Settlement, demography, subsistence hinterland, and territory at first millennium BCE Knossos in its Central Cretan context. In F. Fadelli and Q. Drillat, eds., *Borders in First Millennium BC Crete: Proceedings of the International Workshop, Athens 20–21 January 2023* Crete (ASAtene Suppl. 16). Rome: Scuola Archeologica Italiana di Atene, 47–82.

Popham, M. R., Calligas, P. G., and Sackett, L. H., eds. (1993). *Lefkandi II.2: The Protogeometric Building at Toumba: The Excavation, Architecture and Finds*. London: British School of Archaeology at Athens.

Popham, M. R., Sackett, L. H., and Themelis, P. G., eds. (1980). *Lefkandi I: The Iron Age* (BSA Supplementary volume 11). London: British School of Archaeology at Athens.

Pratt, C. E. (2021). *Oil, Wine, and the Cultural Economy of Ancient Greece: From the Bronze Age to the Archaic Era*. Cambridge, New York, Melbourne, New Delhi, Singapore: Cambridge University Press.

Pratt, C. E. (2025). *Economy and Commodity Production in the Aegean Bronze Age* (Cambridge Elements: Elements in the Aegean Bronze Age). Cambridge and New York: Cambridge University Press.

Prent, M. (2005). *Cretan Sanctuaries and Cults: Continuity and Change from Late Minoan IIIC to the Archaic Period*. Leiden and Boston: Brill.

Preston Day, L., Gesell, G. C., Dierckx, H. M. C. et al. (2016). *Kavousi IIC: The Late Minoan IIIC Settlement at Vronda: Specialist Reports and Analyses* (Prehistory Monographs 52). Philadelphia, PA: INSTAP Academic Press.

Preston Day, L. and Liston, M. A. (2023). *Kavousi IV. The Early Iron Age Cemeteries at Vronda* (Prehistory Monographs, 71). Bristol: INSTAP Academic Press.

Pullen, D. J. (2022). Shaping a Mycenaean cultural landscape at Kalamianos, Greece. In A. Brysbaert, I. Vikatou, and J. Pakkanen, eds., *Shaping Cultural Landscapes: Connecting Agriculture, Crafts, Construction, Transport, and Resilience Strategies*. Leiden: Sidestone Press, pp. 187–204.

Renfrew, C. (1972). *The Emergence of Civilization: The Cyclades and the Aegean in the Third Millennium b.c.* London: Methuen.

Renfrew, C. (1985). *The Archaeology of Cult: The Sanctuary at Phylakopi* (BSA Supplementary Colume 18). London: British School at Athens.

Rönnberg M. (2021). *Athen und Attika vom 11. bis zum frühen 6. Jh. v. Chr. Siedlungsgeschichte, politische Institutionalisierungs- und gesellschaftliche Formierungsprozesse* (Tübinger Archäologische Forschungen 33). Rahden: Marie Leidorf.

Rose, C. B. and Darbyshire, G. (2011). *The New Chronology of Iron Age Gordion* (Gordion Special Studies, 6). Philadelphia: University of Pennsylvania Museum of Archaeology and Anthropology.

Rousioti, D. P. (2018). *Ιερά και θρησκευτικές τελετουργίες στην ανακτορική και μετανακτορική Μυκηναϊκή περίοδο*. Athens: Maistros.

Ruppenstein, F. (2013). Cremation burials in Greece from the Late Bronze Age to the Early Iron Age: Continuity or change? In M. Lochner and F. Ruppenstein, eds., *Brandbestattungen von der mittleren Donau bis zur Ägäis zwischen 1300 und 750 v. Chr: Akten des internationalen Symposiums an der Österreichischen Akademie der Wissenschaften in Wien, 11.–12. Februar 2010*. Wien: Verlag der Österreichischen Akademie der Wissenschaften, pp. 185–96.

Ruppenstein, F. (2020). Migration events in Greece at the end of the second millennium BC and their possible Balkanic background. In J. Maran, R. Băjenaru, S.-C. Ailincăi, A.-D. Popescu, and S. Hansen, eds., *Objects, Ideas and Travelers Contacts between the Balkans, the Aegean and Western Anatolia during the Bronze and Early Iron Age: Volume to the Memory of Alexandru Vulpe*. Bonn: Dr. Rudolf Habelt, pp. 107–22.

Rutherford, I. (2013). Mycenaean religion. In M. Salzman, ed., *The Cambridge History of Religions in the Ancient World*, Vol. 1. Cambridge: Cambridge University Press, pp. 256–79.

Rutter, J. (1992). Cultural novelties in the Post-Palatial Aegean world: Indices of vitality or decline? In W. A. Ward and M. S. Joukowsky, eds., *The Crisis Years: The 12th Century B.C.: From beyond the Danube to the Tigris*. Dubuque, IA: Kendall/Hunt, pp. 61–78.

Sandars, N. (1964). The last Mycenaeans and the European Late Bronze Age. *Antiquity* **38**, 258–62.

Sandars, N. K. (1978). *The Sea Peoples: Warriors of the Ancient Mediterranean, 1250–1150 BC*. London: Thames and Hudson.

Santini, M. (2022). *A Common Path in a Diverse World: Political Development in the Iron Age Eastern Mediterranean, ca. 1200–600 BC*. Ph.D. dissertation. University of Princeton.

Schepartz, L., Stocker, S. R., Davis, J. L. et al. (2017). Mycenaean hierarchy and gender roles: Diet and health inequalities in Late Bronze Age Pylos, Greece. In H. D. Klaus, A. R. Harvey, and M. N. Cohan, eds., *Bones of Complexity: Bioarchaeological Case Studies of Social Organization and Skeletal Biology*. Gainesville: University of Florida Press, pp. 141–72.

Sherratt, S. (1998). Sea Peoples and the economic structure of the late second millennium in the eastern Mediterranean. In S. Gitin, A. Mazar, and E. Stern, eds., *Mediterranean Peoples in Transition: Thirteenth to Early Tenth Centuries BCE: In Honor of Professor Trude Dothan*. Jerusalem: Israel Exploration Society, pp. 292–313.

Sherratt, S. (2004). Feasting in Homeric epic. *Hesperia* **73**(2), 301–37.

Sherratt, S. (2013). The ceramic phenomenon of the "Sea Peoples": An overview. In A. Killebrew and G. Lehmann, eds., *The Philistines and Other "Sea Peoples" in Text and Archaeology*. Atlanta: Society of Biblical Literature, pp. 619–44.

Sherratt, S. (2020). From the Near East to the Far West. In I. S. Lemos and A. Kotsonas, eds., *A Companion to the Archaeology of Early Greece and the Mediterranean*. Hoboken, NJ: Wiley Blackwell, pp. 187–215.

Sherratt, E. (2023). Greek silver before coinage: Medium of exchange, means of wealth accumulation, or commodity? In T. Wilkinson and E. Sherratt, eds., *Circuits of Metal Value: Changing Roles of Metals in the Early Aegean and nearby Lands*. Oxford: Oxbow, pp. 54–76.

Sherratt, S. and Sherratt, A. (1992–3). The growth of the Mediterranean economy in the early first millennium BC. *World Archaeology* **24**, 361–78.

Skeat, T. C. (1934). *The Dorians in Archaeology*. London: Alexander Moring.

Sloan, R. E. and Duncan, M. A. (1978). Zooarchaeology of Nichoria. In G., Jr. Rapp and S. E. Aschenbrenner, eds., *Excavations at Nichoria in Southwest Greece I. Site, Environs, and Techniques*, Vol. I. Minneapolis: University of Minnesota Press, pp. 60–77.

Small, D. (2011). Contexts, agency, and social change in ancient Greece. In N. Terrenato and D. Haggis, eds., *State Formation in Italy and Greece: Questioning the Neoevolutionist Paradigm*. Oxford: Oxbow Books, pp. 197–217.

Snodgrass, A. M. (1971). *The Dark Age of Greece: An Archaeological Survey of the Eleventh to the Eighth Centuries BC*. Edinburgh: Edinburgh University Press.

Snodgrass, A. M. (1977). *Archaeology and the Rise of the Greek State: An Inaugural Lecture*. Cambridge: Cambridge University Press.

Snodgrass, A. (1980a). *Archaic Greece: The Age of Experiment*. London – Melbourne – Toronto: J. M. Dent and Sons.

Snodgrass, A. M. (1980b). Iron and early metallurgy in the Mediterranean. In T. A. Wertime and J. D. Muhly, eds., *The Coming of the Age of Iron*. New Haven, CT: Yale University Press, pp. 335–75.

Snodgrass, A. (1987). *An Archaeology of Greece: The Present State and Future Scope of a Discipline*. Berkeley, Los Angeles, London: University of California Press.

Snodgrass, A. M. (2002). The rejection of Mycenaean culture and the Oriental connection. In E. A. Braun-Holzinger and H. Matthäus, eds., *Die nahöstlichen Kulturen und Griechenland ander Wende vom 2. zum 1. Jahrtausend v. Chr*. Möhnesee-Wamel: Bibliopolis, pp. 1–9.

Sourvinou-Inwood, C. (1993). Early sanctuaries, the eighth century and ritual space: Fragments of a discourse. In N. Marinatos and R. Hägg, eds., *Greek Sanctuaries: New Approaches*. London and New York: Routledge, pp. 1–17.

Stampolidis, N. C., ed. (2001). *Πρακτικά του Συμποσίου Καύσεις στην Εποχή του Χαλκού και την Πρώιμη Εποχή του Σιδήρου, Rhodes, 29 April – 2 May 1999*. Athens: University of Crete and KB', EKPA.

Stampolidis, N. C., ed. (2003). *Sea Routes ... From Sidon to Huelva: Interconnections in the Mediterranean, 16th–6th c. BC*. Athens: Museum of Cycladic Art.

Stampolidis, N. C., ed. (2012). *"Princesses" of the Mediterranean in the Dawn of History*. Athens: Museum of Cycladic Art.

Stissi, V. (2011). Finding the Early Iron Age in field survey: Two case-studies from Boeotia and Magnesia. In K. Reber, S. Verdan, A. Kenzelmann-Pfyffer, and T. Theurillat, eds., *Early Iron Age Pottery: A Quantitative Approach: Round Table Organized by the Swiss School of Archaeology in Greece in Collaboration with the University of Lausanne*. Oxford: Archaeopress, pp. 149–62.

Stockhammer, P. W. (2024). The collapse of the Mycenaean palaces revisited. In A. Yasur-Landau, G. Gambash, and T. E. Levy, eds., *Mediterranean Resilience: Collapse and Adaptation in Antique Maritime Societies*. Sheffield and Bristol: Equinox, pp. 115–27.

Tandy, D. W. (1997). *Warriors into Traders: The Power of the Market in Early Greece*. Berkeley: University of California Press.

Tarlow, S. and Nilsson Stutz, L. eds., (2013). *The Oxford Handbook of the Archaeology of Death and Burial*. Oxford: Oxford University Press.

Thaler, U. (2020). Architecture. In I. S. Lemos and A. Kotsonas, eds., *A Companion to the Archaeology of Early Greece and the Mediterranean*. Hoboken, NJ: Wiley Blackwell, pp. 377–406.

Thomas, C. G. and Conant, C. eds. (1999). *Citadel to City-State: The Transformation of Greece, 1200–700 B.C.E*. Bloomington and Indianapolis: Indiana University Press.

Thomatos, M. (2006). *The Final Revival of the Aegean Bronze Age: A Case Study of the Argolid, Corinthia, Attica, Euboea, the Cyclades and the Dodecanese during LH IIIC Middle*. Oxford: Archaeopress.

Toffolo, M. B., Fantalkin, A., Lemos, I. S. et al. (2013). Towards an absolute chronology for the Aegean Iron Age: New radiocarbon dates from Lefkandi, Kalapodi and Corinth. *PLoS ONE* **8**(12), e83117. https://doi.org/10.1371/journal.pone.0083117.

Tournavitou, I. (2023). Mycenaean architecture and the assimilation of the palatial model. In B. F. Steinmann, J. Maran, and D. Panagiotopoulos, eds.,

Ambivalent Times: The Mycenaean Palatial Period between Splendour and Demise. Bonn: Dr. Rudolf Habelt, pp. 1–34.

Triantafyllou, S. (2025). *The Use of Fire on Human Remains in Prehistory and Protohistory. Final Meeting of the TEFRA Project*, Thessaloniki, May 24–25.

Vago, S. (2004). *Social Change*, 5th ed. Upper Saddle River, NJ: Prentice Hall.

Valavanis P. (2020). Αρματοδρομία και συμπόσιο στη μετανακτορική Τίρυνθα. In *ΚΥΔΑΛΙΜΟΣ. Τιμητικός τόμος για τον καθηγητή Γεώργιο Στυλ. Κορρέ, Τόμος 1* (AURA Supplement 4). Athens: University of Athens, pp. 285–95.

Van Damme, T. M. (2017). *Life after the Palaces: A Household Archaeology Approach to Mainland Greece during Late Helladic IIIC*. Ph.D. dissertation. University of California Los Angeles.

Van Damme, T. and Lis, B. (2024). The origin of the Protogeometric style in northern Greece and its relevance for the absolute chronology of the Early Iron Age. *Antiquity* **98**(401), 1271–89. https://doi.org/10.15184/aqy.2024.144.

Van den Berg, K. A. M. (2018). *Keeping in Touch in a Changing World: Network Dynamics and the Connections between the Aegean and Italy during the Bronze Age – Iron Age Transition (ca. 1250 – 1000 BC)*. Ph.D. dissertation. Free University, Amsterdam.

van der Plicht, H., Bruins, H. J., and Nijboer, A. J. (2009). The Iron Age around the Mediterranean: A high chronology perspective from the Groningen radiocarbon database. *Radiocarbon* **51**, 213–42.

van Wijngaarden, G. J. and Driessen, J., eds. (2022). *Political Geographies of the Bronze Age Aegean: Proceedings of the Joint Workshop by the Belgian School at Athens (EBSA) and the Netherlands Institute at Athens (NIA), May 28 to 31, 2019* (Babesch Supplementa 43). Leuven: Peeters.

Vaxevanopoulos, M., Blichert-Toft, J., Davis, G., and Albarède, F. (2022). New findings of ancient Greek silver sources. *JAS* **137**, 1–27.

Vermeule, E. (1960). The fall of the Mycenaean empire. *Archaeology* **13**(1), 66–76.

Vermeule, E. (1979). *Aspects of Death in Early Greek Art and Poetry*. Berkeley: University of California Press.

Vlachou, V. (2024). Interpreting the pottery deposits from the Spartan Amyklaion: Providing a framework for the early stages of cult and ritual. In M. Kerschner, ed., *Interpreting the Pottery Record from Geometric and Archaic Sanctuaries in the Northwestern Peloponnese: Proceedings of the International Online Symposium, November 5–6, 2020*. Vienna: Austrian Academy of Sciences, pp. 321–45.

Waldbaum, J. C. (1978). *From Bronze to Iron: The Transition from the Bronze Age to the Iron Age in the Eastern Mediterranean* (Studies in Mediterranean Archaeology, 54). Göteborg: Paul Åström Förlag.

Wallace, S. (2010). *Ancient Crete: From Successful Collapse to Democracy's Alternatives, Twelfth to Fifth Centuries BC*. Cambridge: Cambridge University Press.

Wallace, S. (2021). Socioeconomic crisis and cultural innovation: The LBA-EIA East Mediterranean via a case study of Lasithi, Crete. *OJA* **40** (4), 391–416.

Walløe, L. (1999). Was the disruption of the Mycenaean world caused by repeated epidemics of bubonic plague? *Opuscula Atheniensia* **24**, 121–6.

Wardle K., Higham T., and Kromer B. (2014). Dating the end of the Greek Bronze Age: A robust radiocarbon-based chronology from Assiros Toumba. *PLoS ONE* **9**(9), e106672. https://doi.org/10.1371/journal.pone.0106672.

Warren, P. M. and Hankey, V. (1989). *Aegean Bronze Age Chronology*. Bristol: Bristol Classical Press.

Weiberg, E., Bevan, A., Kouli, K. et al. (2019). Long-term trends of land use and demography in Greece: A comparative study. *Holocene* **29**(5), 742–60.

Weiberg, E. and Finné, M. (2018). Resilience and persistence of ancient societies in the face of climate change: A case study from Late Bronze Age Peloponnese. *World Archaeology* **50**, 584–602.

Welton, L., Harrison, T., Batiuk, S. et al. (2019). Shifting networks and community identity at Tell Tayinat in the Iron I (ca. 12th to mid 10th century B.C.E.). *AJA* **123**(2), 291–333.

Weninger, B. and Jung, R. (2009). Absolute chronology of the end of the Aegean Bronze Age. In S. Deger-Jalkotzy and A. E. Bächle, eds., *LH III C Chronology and Synchronisms III: LH III C Late and the Transition to the Early Iron Age. Proceedings of the International Workshop Held at the Austrian Academy of Sciences at Vienna, February 23rd and 24th, 2007*. Wien: Verlag der Österreichischen Akademie der Wissenschaft, pp. 373–416.

Whitelaw, T. (2000). Beyond the palace: A century of investigation in Europe's oldest city. *BICS* **44**, 223–26.

Whitley, J. (1991a). *Style and Society in Dark Age Greece: The Changing Face of a Pre-Literate Society 1100–700 bc*. Cambridge: Cambridge University Press.

Whitley, J. (1991b). Social diversity in Dark Age Greece. *BSA* **86**, 341–65.

Whitley, J. (1996). Gender and hierarchy in early Athens: The strange case of the disappearance of the rich female grave. *Metis* **11**, 209–32.

Whitley, J. (2001). *The Archaeology of Ancient Greece*. Cambridge: Cambridge University Press.

Whitley, J. (2002). Objects with attitude: Biographical facts and fallacies in the study of Late Bronze Age and Early Iron Age warrior graves. *CAJ* **12**, 217–32.

Whitley, J. (2009). The chimera of continuity: What would "continuity of cult" actually demonstrate? In A. L. D'Agata, A. van de Moortel, and M. B. Richardson, eds., *Archaeologies of Cult: Essays on Ritual and Cult in Crete in Honor of Geraldine C. Gesell* (Hesperia Supplement 42). Princeton, NJ: American School of Classical Studies at Athens, pp. 279–88.

Whitley, J. (2012). Homer's entangled objects: Narrative, agency and personhood in and out of Iron Age texts. *CArchJ* **23**, 395–416.

Whitley, J. (2016). Burning people, breaking things: Material entanglements, the Bronze Age/Iron Age transition and the Homeric dividual. In M. Mina, S. Triantaphyllou, and Y. Papadatos, eds., *An Archaeology of Prehistoric Bodies and Embodied Identities in the Eastern Mediterranean*. Oxbow Books: Philadelphia, pp. 215–23.

Whittaker, H. (1997). *Mycenaean Cult Buildings: A Study of their Architecture and Function in the Context of the Aegean and the Eastern Mediterranean* (Monographs from the Norwegian Institute at Athens 1). Bergen: Norwegian Institute at Athens.

Wiener, M. (2017). Causes of complex collapse at the end of the Bronze Age. In P. M. Fischer and T. Bürge, eds., *"Sea Peoples" Up-to-Date: New Research on Transformations in the Eastern Mediterranean in the 13th–11th centuries BCE*. Vienna: Österreichische Akademie der Wissenschaften, pp. 43–74.

Wiersma, C. W. and Voutsaki, S., eds. (2016). *Social Change in Aegean Prehistory*. Oxford and Philadelphia: Oxbow Books.

Williams, E. W. (1962). The end of an epoch. *Greece and Rome* **9**(2), 109–25.

Wright, J. C. (1994). The spatial configuration of belief: The archaeology of Mycenaean religion. In S. Alcock and R. Osborne, eds., *Placing the Gods: Sanctuaries and Sacred Space in Ancient Greece*. Oxford and New York: Clarendon Press and Oxford University Press, pp. 37–78.

Zurbach, J. (2017). *Les hommes, la terre et la dette en Grèce, c. 1400–c. 500 a.C.* (Scripta Antiqua 95). Bordeaux: Ausonius Éditions.

Acknowledgements

I thank the editors for the invitation, and the reviewers and Dominic Pollard for their feedback. The work is dedicated to Todd Whitelaw, for generously sharing his advice with me on Knossos and the Aegean Bronze Age over the last fifteen years .

Cambridge Elements

The Aegean Bronze Age

Carl Knappett
University of Toronto
Carl Knappett is the Walter Graham/ Homer Thompson Chair in Aegean Prehistory at the University of Toronto.

Irene Nikolakopoulou
Hellenic Ministry of Culture, Archaeological Museum of Heraklion
Irene Nikolakopoulou is an archaeologist and curator at the Archaeological Museum of Heraklion, Crete.

About the Series
This series is devised thematically to foreground the conceptual developments in the Aegean Bronze Age, one of the richest subfields of archaeology, while reflecting the range of institutional settings in which research in this field is conducted. It aims to produce an innovative and comprehensive review of the latest scholarship in Aegean prehistory.

Cambridge Elements

The Aegean Bronze Age

Elements in the Series

Long-Distance Exchange and Inter-Regional Economies
Sarah C. Murray

Aegeomania: Modern Reimaginings of the Aegean Bronze Age
Nicoletta Momigliano

Economy and Commodity Production in the Aegean Bronze Age
Catherine E. Pratt

The Emergence of Aegean Prehistory
Andrew Shapland

Social Change across the End of the Aegean Bronze Age
Antonis Kotsonas

A full series listing is available at: www.cambridge.org/EABA

For EU product safety concerns, contact us at Calle de José Abascal, 56–1º,
28003 Madrid, Spain or eugpsr@cambridge.org.

www.ingramcontent.com/pod-product-compliance
Lightning Source LLC
LaVergne TN
LVHW011852060526
838200LV00054B/4284